1000 things you should know about

birds

D1294347

1000 things you should know about

birds

Jinny Johnson
Consultant: Steve Parker

Miles Kelly
PUBLISHING

First published in 2005 by Miles Kelly Publishing Ltd
Bardfield Centre, Great Bardfield, Essex, CM7 4SL

Copyright © Miles Kelly Publishing Ltd 2005

This title is also available in hardback

2 4 6 8 10 9 7 5 3 1

Editorial Director: Belinda Gallagher
Picture Researchers: Liberty Newton, Bethany Walker
Production Manager: Estela Boulton **Designed and Edited:** Starry Dog Books
Cover Designer: Tony Collins

British Library Cataloguing-in-Publication Data
A catalogue record for this book is available from the British Library

ISBN 1-84236-632-7

Printed in China

info@mileskelly.net
visit us at our website: www.mileskelly.net

CONTENTS

KEY

 How birds live

 Perching birds

 Owls and birds of prey

 Water and wading birds

 Game and ground birds

 Woodland and forest birds

The world of birds

- **There are more than 9000 species** of birds.

- **One of the most widespread** of all birds is the osprey, which is found nearly all over the world.

- **More than a third of all known bird species** live and breed in South and Central America.

▲ *Ospreys make a large nest at the top of a tree or on a cliff. They feed mostly on fish, which they snatch up with their feet.*

- **A species** is a particular type of bird. Birds of the same species can mate and have young, and these can themselves have offspring.

- **The 9000 bird species** are organized into about 180 families. Species in a family share certain characteristics such as body shape.

- **Bird families** are organized into 28 or 29 larger groups called orders. Largest is the perching bird order, with more than 5000 bird species.

- **The wandering albatross** is one of the longest-lived birds. Individuals may live as long as 50 years.

- **The red-billed quelea** is probably the most common wild bird. There are thought to be at least 1.5 billion.

- **The largest bird**, the ostrich, weighs almost 80,000 times more than the smallest, the bee hummingbird.

- **All birds** lay hard-shelled eggs, in which their young develop. If a mother bird had young that developed inside her body instead, she would be too heavy to fly.

Cormorants and anhingas

- **The 4 species of anhinga** also called darters all live in freshwater in tropical parts of the world.

- **The flightless cormorant** lives on two of the Galapagos Islands. Its tiny wings are useless for flight, but it is an expert swimmer.

- **The feathers** of cormorants and darters lack waterproofing and quickly get soaked through. This makes the birds heavier in water and better able to dive for fish.

- **After diving for food**, cormorants stand on a rock with wings outstretched to dry.

▶ *The cormorant's long, hooked beak is an ideal shape for catching fish, its main food.*

- **In parts of Asia**, fishermen use cormorants to catch fish – the birds dive for the fish but do not swallow them.

- **Cormorant colonies** may number 100,000 birds or more. Their droppings, known as guano, are collected and used as fertilizer.

- **The biggest species** of cormorant, the great cormorant, is up to 1 m long.

- **A great cormorant eats** about 15% of its body weight in fish a day. That's like an adult human eating more than 80 hamburgers a day.

- **The American darter**, or snake bird, swims with its neck held in a snakelike curve above the water's surface.

★ STAR FACT ★
Cormorants can dive to an incredible 50 m or more in their hunt for fish.

Ducks

- **The female eider duck** lines her nest with soft down feathers that she pulls from her breast. Humans use the feathers, too, to make quilts and sleeping bags.

- **Torrent ducks** live by fast-flowing streams in South America's Andes mountains. When new ducklings hatch, they leap straight into the swirling waters.

- **There are more than 100 duck species**, living all over the world, except Antarctica.

- **Steamer ducks** get their name from their habit of paddling over water with their wings as well as their feet, at speeds of up to 28 km/h.

- **Ducks have been domesticated** for more than 2000 years for their meat and eggs.

- **Ducks** feed on fish, shellfish, leaves and seeds.

- **Like cuckoos**, the black-headed duck lays its eggs in the nests of other birds, such as herons.

- **The merganser** has a serrated beak like the blade of a bread knife, to help it hold slippery fish.

- **The wood duck** was hunted nearly to extinction in the 19th century for the male's colourful feathers, which were used as fishing flies and hat decorations.

- **The red-breasted merganser** is one of the fastest-flying birds. It can reach speeds of more than 65 km/h – and possibly even 100 km/h.

▼ The beautiful wood duck breeds in North America.

Hoopoes and relatives

- **Rollers** have a spectacular courtship flight, rolling and somersaulting as they dive towards land.

- **The 8 noisy, insect-eating woodhoopoe species** live in forests in central and southern Africa.

- **A light, coin-shaped mark** on each wing of the broad-billed roller is the reason for its other common name – 'dollar bird'.

- **The cuckoo-roller** lives only in Madagascar and the Comoros

Islands, where it catches chameleons and insects.

- **Groups of woodhoopoes** make loud calls and rocking movements, and pass bark to each other, in a display of territorial ownership.

- **The 16 or so species of roller** and ground roller live in southern Europe, Asia, Africa and Australia.

- **The broad-billed roller** catches winged termites in the air. A roller will eat as many as 800 termites an evening.

- **If threatened** by birds of prey, the hoopoe hides by flattening itself on the ground with its wings and tail spread out.

- **The hoopoe** was a symbol of gratitude in ancient Egyptian hieroglyphics. The Egyptians believed that the hoopoe comforted its parents in their old age.

- **The hoopoe lines its nest** with animal excrement, perhaps so that the smell will keep enemies away!

◀ With its decorative crest and striking plumage, the hoopoe is easy to recognize. It lives in Europe, Asia and Africa.

Starlings

- **The male wattled starling** loses his head feathers in the breeding season. Scientists investigating cures for human baldness are researching the bird's ability to regrow its head feathers each year.

- **When kept in captivity**, hill mynahs mimic human speech, but wild birds do not imitate the calls of other bird species, only the calls of other hill mynahs.

- **The largest starlings** are up to 43 cm long and weigh just over 100 g.

- **European starlings** feed their young on caterpillars, earthworms and beetle

▶ *The male starling has glossy, iridescent plumage. The female is much plainer, with brownish feathers.*

grubs, and may make 400 feeding trips a day.

- **Male starlings** bring fresh green leaves to the nest, which release a substance that deters parasites.

- **The Brahminy starling** has a brush-like tip on its tongue, used for collecting pollen and nectar.

- **There are about 113 species of starling** in Europe, Africa and Asia. Starlings have also been introduced into Australasia and North America.

- **Some 100 years ago,** 60 pairs of European starlings were released in New York. Fifty years later, starlings were one of the most common birds in the USA.

- **Locusts** are the favourite food of the rose-coloured starling. Large flocks fly to wherever they are plentiful.

★ STAR FACT ★
In some cities, flocks of as many as 1 million starlings gather for the night.

The structure of birds

- **Birds are the only creatures** to have feathers. These keep them warm and protected from the weather and allow them to fly.

- **Like mammals, fish and reptiles**, a bird is a vertebrate animal – it has a backbone.

- **Birds** have a body temperature of 40°C to 44°C – higher than other warm-blooded animals.

- **A bird's bones** have a honeycomb structure. The bones are so light that they account for only about 5% of its total weight.

- **Birds** do not have teeth. Instead their food is ground down by a

▲ *Thrushes are adaptable birds, able to feed on fruit as well as insects. Many have beautiful songs.*

part of the digestive system called the gizzard. Some birds swallow small stones to help the action of the gizzard.

- **A bird's nostrils** are usually at the base of the beak, but in the kiwi, which has a better sense of smell than most birds, they are at the tip.

- **Birds' muscles** make up 30–60% of their total weight. The biggest are the flight and leg muscles.

- **Small birds** have about 15 neck vertebrae, while the mute swan has 23. (Mammals have only 7.)

- **The skeleton** of a bird's wings has bones similar to those in the hand and arm of mammals, but there are much reduced bones for only three fingers not five.

- **The heart rate** of a tiny hummingbird reaches an astonishing 615 beats a minute.

Swifts

- **Once a young swift** has left its nest, it may not come to land again until it is about 2 years old and ready to breed. In this time it may fly 500,000 km.

- **The edible-nest swiftlet** makes a nest of its own spit (saliva) and a few feathers on a cave wall. Birds nest soup made from this nest is considered a delicacy in China

- **Swifts** do almost everything in the air. They eat, drink, court and even mate on the wing.

- **There are about 74 species of swifts** found all over the world, except in the very far north and south.

- **The largest swift**, the white-naped swift, is about 25 cm long and weighs 175 g – about the weight of a lemon.

- **Trials with ringed birds** have shown that a young common swift that has only just left the nest can fly from London to Madrid in 3 days.

- **A swift's legs** and feet are so small and weak that it cannot move on the ground. It must land on a cliff ledge or building so it can launch itself into the air again.

- **The cave swiftlet** finds its way in totally dark caves by using a form of echolocation.

- **The African palm swift** glues its nest to the underneath of a palm leaf with its own spit, and glues its eggs to the nest. The parents cling on with their claws while incubating the clutch.

- **When a swift regurgitates** a mouthful of food for its young to eat, it may contain as many as 1000 tiny insects and spiders.

◀ *The Eurasian swift is seen in Europe in the summer, swooping overhead on sunny days. It flies to tropical Africa for the winter.*

Partridges and relatives

- **The Himalayan snowcock** (partridge family) lives on the lower slopes of the Himalayas, where its grey and white feathers hide it among rocks and snow.

- **Tiny quail chicks** are born with their eyes open and their bodies covered in warm, downy feathers. They are able to follow their mother within 1 hour of hatching.

- **A mother quail** helps her chicks to learn how to find food by pointing at food items with her beak.

- **At about 50 cm long**, the vulturine guineafowl is the largest of the 6 species of guineafowl. It lives in Africa and eats fallen fruit.

- **The female red-legged partridge** lays one clutch of eggs for her mate to incubate, and another to incubate herself.

- **The partridge family** includes more than 90 species of partridges and francolins. They feed mainly on seeds.

- **In parts of Europe and North America**, partridges are reared in captivity and then released and shot for sport.

- **The helmeted guineafowl**, originally from Africa, was domesticated in Europe more than 2500 years ago.

- **A group of partridges** is called a 'covey'. A covey usually contains a family of male, female and young, plus a few other birds.

- **The grey partridge** lays the largest clutch of any bird – on average about 19 or 20 eggs, but some birds lay as many as 25.

◀ *The crested wood partridge lives in woodland and forest in Southeast Asia. It feeds on insects, snails, fruit and seeds.*

Birds of paradise

- **Birds of paradise**, of which there are about 44 species, live only in New Guinea and northeastern Australia.
- **The king of Saxony** bird of paradise has two 50 cm head plumes decorated with small, sky-blue squares, so unusual-looking they were first thought to be fake.
- **The magnificent riflebird** gets its name from its loud whistling call, which sounds like a passing bullet.
- The **Female bird** makes a cup or dome-shaped nest and lays 1–2 eggs.
- **During courtship**, the blue bird of paradise hangs upside-down from a branch with his splendid blue feathers and tail plumes spread over his head.
- **Fruit and insects** are the main foods of

◀ *The blue bird of paradise is one of the rarer birds of the species.*

★ **STAR FACT** ★
The tail feathers of the male ribbon-tailed bird of paradise are up to 1 m long.

the birds of paradise. Some also eat leaves and buds.

- **New Guinea tribesmen** traditionally wear bird of paradise feathers in their head-dresses.
- **During the early 19th century**, 100,000 bird of paradise skins were sold each year in Europe for hat and dress decorations.
- **The first bird of paradise skins** brought to Europe from New Guinea did not have feet, so some people thought the birds never landed.

▶ *The male king bird of paradise has long tail feathers for display.*

Geese and swans

- **Whooper, trumpeter and mute swans** are among the heaviest flying birds, weighing up to 16 kg.
- **Snow geese** breed in the Arctic tundra, but fly south to spend the winter months around the Gulf of Mexico – a journey of some 3500 km.
- **The black swan** makes a nest of sticks and other plant material in shallow water and lays up to 6 eggs. Both parents help to incubate the eggs.
- **Geese** feed mostly on leaves, and can eat as many as 100 blades of grass in 1 minute.
- **Tundra swans** mate for life, returning year after year to the same nesting site. They usually make their nest on marshland and lay 3–5 eggs.
- **Although quieter than other swans**, the mute swan is not really

★ **STAR FACT** ★
Bar-headed geese have been seen flying near the top of Mount Everest, at 8848 m high.

mute, but makes many snorting and hissing calls.

- **The Hawaiian goose** is the world's rarest goose. Fifty years ago there were only about 30 left. Now it is protected and numbers are increasing.
- **Red-breasted geese** often make their nests near those of peregrines and buzzards. This gives them protection, and they don't seem to get attacked by the birds of prey.
- **Male swans** are known as 'cobs', females as 'pens' and baby swans are called 'cygnets'.

▼ *Swans generally stay faithful to one mate.*

Tyrant flycatchers

- **The tyrant flycatcher family** includes at least 390 species of birds. They range from northern Canada through the USA to the tip of South America.

- **Not all flycatchers** feed only on insects. The great kiskadee dives into water for fish and tadpoles, as well as catching flying insects in the air.

- **The vermilion flycatcher** is one of the few brightly coloured flycatchers. The male has bright red plumage, which it shows off in his courtship display.

- **In 1976**, ornithologists – bird-watchers – in Peru found a previously unknown flycatcher, which they named the cinnamon-breasted tody-tyrant. It lives only in cloud forests on a few mountain peaks in Peru.

- **The royal flycatcher** is a plain, brownish bird, but it has an amazing crest of feathers on its head that it sometimes unfurls and shows off. Males have red crests and females yellow or orange crests.

- **Smallest of all the tyrant flycatchers** is the short-tailed pygmy tyrant, at only 6.5 cm long. It lives in northern South America.

▶ The vermilion flycatcher brings a flash of colour to the desert and dry scrub of the southwestern USA, Central America and tropical South America.

- **The eastern phoebe** makes a nest of mud mixed with grass and plant stems. The female lays 3–7 eggs, and incubates them for 14–16 days. The young leave the nest when they are about 17 days old.

- **The boat-billed flycatcher** has a larger beak than other flycatchers, and eats frogs and other small animals, as well as insects.

- **Some flycatchers**, including the great crested flycatcher, line their nests with snakeskins that have been cast off.

▲ The tyrant flycatchers are the largest bird family in North and South America. Shown here are: (1) the buff-breasted flycatcher, (2) the lesser flycatcher and (3) the great-crested flycatcher.

★ STAR FACT ★
Well-known for its fierce behaviour, the eastern kingbird (a flycatcher) attacks larger birds that dare to approach its territory, sometimes even landing on their backs.

Nightjars and relatives

- **After hunting** for insects at night, the common potoo rests by day in a tree, where its position and coloration make it look like a broken branch.

- **The 12 species of frogmouth** live in the rainforests of Southeast Asia and Australia.

- **The common poorwill** (nightjar family) is one of the few birds known to hibernate. It sleeps in a rock crevice.

- **The bristle-fringed beak** of the nightjar opens very wide to help it snap up moths and beetles at night.

- **The oilbird** is the only bird to feed

◄ *The potoo lives in forests and woodlands in Mexico and Central and South America.*

> ★ **STAR FACT** ★
> So as not to give themselves away by their droppings, potoos squirt out their faeces so that they land well away from their perches.

on fruit at night. Its excellent sense of smell helps it find the oily fruits of palms and laurels in the dark.

- **Oilbird chicks** put on so much weight from their rich diet that they may weigh much more than their parents when they are only a couple of months old.

- **There are about 70 species of nightjars**, found in most warmer parts of the world except New Zealand and southern South America.

- **The oilbird** nests in dark caves, and uses echolocation.

- **An old name** for nightjars is goatsuckers, because people mistakenly thought they saw the birds feeding on goats' milk, when in fact they were snapping up insects disturbed by the animals.

Oystercatchers and relatives

- **The oystercatcher** uses its strong, bladelike beak to prise mussels off rocks and open their shells.

- **Oystercatcher chicks** stay with their parents for up to 1 year while they learn how to find and open shellfish.

- **The Egyptian plover** (courser family) buries its eggs in sand and leaves them to be incubated by the warmth of the sun. The parents sit on the eggs at night and if the weather is cool.

- **The cream-coloured courser** has pale, sandy feathers that help to keep it hidden in its desert home.

- **The 17 species in the courser and pratincole family**

▶ *The common oystercatcher breeds in Europe and Asia, but spends the winter in South Africa and southern Asia.*

live in southern Europe, Asia, Africa and Australia.

- **The common pratincole** nests on sand or rocks, and lays 2–4 mottled, well-camouflaged eggs. The parents take turns to incubate the eggs for 17–18 days.

- **The 9 species in the thick-knee family** include the stone curlew and the dikkop. These long-legged birds usually feed at night on insects, worms and shellfish.

- **The thick-knees** get their common name from the knobbly joints on their legs – actually between the ankle and shin bones.

- **If the Egyptian plover's chicks** get too hot, the parent birds soak their own belly feathers with water and give their young a cooling shower.

- **The pygmy seed-snipe** of southern South America blends in with the plains landscape so well that it is almost invisible when it crouches on the ground.

Fairy-wrens and relatives

- **The 26 species of fairy-wrens** live in Australia and New Guinea, where they forage for insects on the ground.

- **Young fairy-wrens** often stay with their parents and help them raise the next brood of young. Pairs with helpers can raise more young than those without.

- **The rock warbler** makes its nest in a dark cave or mine-shaft, attaching the nest to the walls with spiderwebs.

- **During its courtship display**, the male superb fairy-wren may present his mate with a yellow flower petal.

- **If a predator** comes too close to a fairy-wren's nest, the parent birds make a special 'rodent run' away from the nest, squeaking and trailing their tails to confuse and distract the enemy.

- **The 50 or so species of thickhead** live in rainforests and scrub in Southeast Asia and Australasia.

- **The white-throated gerygone's nest** hangs from a eucalyptus branch and is made from bark strips and plant fibres woven together with spiderwebs.

- **The hooded pitohui** (thickhead family) is one of the very few poisonous birds known. Its feathers and skin contain a poison that protects it from predators.

- **The Australasian warbler** family includes 65 species of gerygone, thornbills and scrubwrens.

- **The golden whistler** is probably the most variable of birds – the 70 or more races all have slightly different feather patterns or beak shapes.

◀ *The male superb fairy-wren is easily recognized by the bright blue plumage around its head and neck.*

Beaks and feet

- **No bird** has more than four toes, but some have three and the ostrich has only two.

- **Four-toed birds** have different arrangements of toes: in swifts, all four point forwards; in most perching birds, three point forwards and one backwards; and in parrots, two point forwards and two backwards.

- **A beak** is made up of a bird's projecting jaw bones, covered in a hard horny material.

- **The hyacinth macaw** has one of the most powerful beaks of any bird, strong enough to crack brazil nuts.

- **Webbed feet** make all waterbirds efficient paddlers.

- **The Australian pelican** has the largest beak of any bird, at up to 50 cm long.

★ STAR FACT ★
A baby bird has a spike called an 'egg-tooth' on its beak for breaking its way out of its egg.

- **Nightjars** have the shortest beaks, at 8–10 mm long.

- **A bird stands** on the tips of its toes – the backward bending joint halfway down its leg is the ankle joint.

- **A bird's beak** is extremely sensitive to touch. Birds that probe in the ground for food have extra sensory organs at the beak tip.

▼ *When a chick is ready to hatch, it makes a tiny hole in the shell with its 'egg-tooth' – a process called 'pipping' – and then struggles its way out.*

First tiny hole

Egg cracks

Chick appears

Chick breaks free of egg

Divers and grebes

- **The great crested grebe** is best known for its amazing courtship dance, during which male and female perform a series of movements in water and exchange pieces of weed.

- **At 90 cm long**, the white-billed diver is the largest of the 4 species of diver.

- **The short-winged grebe** lives on lakes high in the mountains of Peru and Bolivia, and cannot fly. It basks in the sun to warm its body after the cold nights.

- **Divers feed only on fish**, which they catch underwater. The great northern diver can dive

◀ The great crested grebe lives in parts of Europe, Asia, Africa and Australasia.

as deep as 20 m or more below the water's surface.

- **In the 19th century**, the breast feathers of grebes were used to make muffs to keep ladies' hands warm.

- **There are about 20 species of grebes** (three flightless). They live near freshwater lakes and marshes.

- **Divers** are so specialized for diving and swimming that adult birds cannot walk upright on land.

- **Grebes** feed on fish, insects and shellfish. They also swallow moulted feathers, which may help them to regurgitate waste such as fish bones and keep their gut free of parasites.

- **The great crested grebe** makes a nest of water plants floating near the water's edge. It lays 3–6 eggs, which both male and female incubate.

Falcons

- **The peregrine** is the fastest bird, diving through the air at 180 km/h to catch prey.

- **The peregrine's hunting technique** is so exacting that only one in ten attacks is successful.

- **At up to 60 cm long**, the gyr falcon is the largest of the falcon family, and can catch ducks and hares.

- **The common kestrel** hovers above the ground on fast-beating wings while it searches for small mammals.

- **Falconets and pygmy falcons** are the smallest birds of prey. The Philippine falconet is only 15 cm long.

- **Falcons** have adapted well to city life – kestrels hover above rubbish bins to watch for mice, and peregrines dive down between New York skyscrapers.

- **Eleonora's falcon** is named after a 14th-century Sardinian princess, who brought in laws to protect it.

- **The earliest known records** of falconry come from 2nd-century BC China.

- **In winter**, both male and female kestrels spend about a quarter of their day hunting. But when the female is incubating eggs, the male hunts for longer.

▲ The peregrine kills with its talons and rips prey apart with its hooked beak.

Parrots

- **The only flightless parrot** is the New Zealand kakapo or owl parrot, which is now extremely rare.

- **The palm cockatoo** has an amazing courtship display. The male bird holds a stick in its foot and makes a loud drumming noise by beating the stick against the side of a tree.

- **At about 85 cm long**, the scarlet macaw of South and Central America is one of the largest of the parrot family.

- **Unlike most parrots**, the kea of New Zealand eats meat as well as fruit and insects. It feasts on carrion – animals that are already dead – and also hunts young shearwaters in their burrows.

- **Macaws nest in tree holes** high in rainforest trees. The female lays two eggs which her mate helps to incubate. The young macaws stay with their parents for up to 2 years

- **The little blue-crowned hanging parrot** gets its name from its strange habit of hanging upside down from a branch when at rest.

- **Macaws** swallow beakfuls of clay from riverbanks. The clay may help to protect the birds from the effects of some plants and seeds that they eat, many of which are poisonous to other creatures.

- **There are about 350 species in the parrot order**, including birds such as macaws, budgerigars, lories and cockatoos. They live in Central and South America, Africa, southern Asia and Australasia

- **As early as 400 BC**, a Greek author wrote of owning a pet parrot – a bird that could speak words in both Indian and Greek!

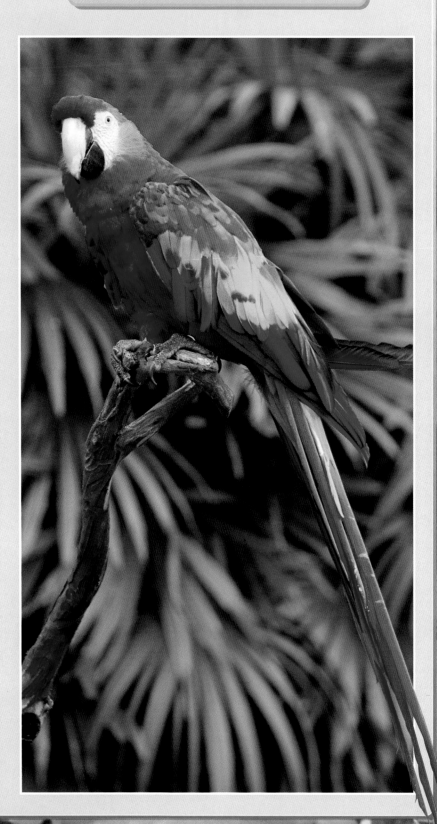

▶ With its bright red feathers, the scarlet macaw is one of the most beautiful of all the parrots. It can fly at up to 56 km/h as it searches the rainforest for fruit, nuts and seeds to eat.

Bird senses

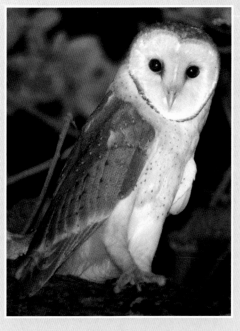

- **Almost all birds** have excellent sight, and most depend on their eyes for finding food.

- **A bird's outer ear** consists of a short tube leading from the eardrum to the outside. In most birds the ear openings are just behind the jaw.

- **A barn owl's hearing** is so good that it can detect and catch prey in complete darkness without using its eyes at all.

- **A chicken** has only 24 tastebuds and a starling about 200 – a human has 9000.

- **An eagle** can spot prey from as much as 1.6 km above the Earth.

- **A starling's eye** is as much as

▲ With its amazing hearing, the barn owl hunts mice and other small rodents at night.

15% of the total weight of its head. A human's eye is only 1% of the head weight.

- **An ostrich's eye**, at 5 cm in diameter, is larger than any other land animal's eye.

- **Birds** are 10 times more sensitive to changes of pitch and intensity in sounds than humans. They can detect sounds of 1/200 second.

- **Kiwis have poor sight** and depend more on their sense of smell for finding many food items, such as earthworms, at night.

- **Albatrosses** have a good sense of smell. In experiments, they have been attracted to food from a distance of 30 km.

Terns and skimmers

- **The noddy**, a species of tern, gets its name from its habit of nodding its head during its courtship display.

- **The black skimmer's beak** has a flattened lower part that is longer than the upper part. The bird flies over water with the lower part of its beak just below the surface, ready to snap up prey.

- **The 42 or so species of terns** are found all over the world, mostly along coasts.

- **Arctic terns** are long-lived birds, known to survive to 27 – and sometimes even 34 – years of age.

- **Most terns eat fish**, squid and shellfish, but marshland terns also eat insects and frogs.

▼ The Arctic tern has a long, forked tail, short red legs and a cap of black feathers on its head.

★ STAR FACT ★
The Arctic tern makes a round-trip migration from the Arctic to Antarctica and back – a record distance of more than 32,000 km.

- **At up to 59 cm long**, the Caspian tern is the largest of the terns, and one of the most widespread.

- **The fairy tern** does not make a nest. Instead, it balances its 1 egg on a tree branch and manages to sit on it without knocking it off.

- **Most terns mate for life**. Even if they don't stay together all year round, pairs meet up when they return to breeding sites.

- **There are only 3 species of skimmers**. most live in coastal areas of tropical Africa, Southeast Asia and North and South America.

Weavers and relatives

- **The sociable weaver** nests in groups of up to 300 birds. The huge nest is made of sticks and grass, and may measure 4 m deep and weigh up to 1000 kg. Each pair of birds has its own hole in the nest.

- **Desert-living sociable weavers** use their nest all year round for shelter from sun, wind and cold. At night, when temperatures drop, the nest holes stay 20°C warmer than the outside air.

- **Whydah birds** do not make their own nests, but lay their eggs in the nests of other birds, usually waxbills.

▶ *When the male cape weaver has finished making a nest, it calls to the female.*

- **Young whydahs** make the same sounds and have the same mouth markings as their foster parents' own young, and because of this they get fed.

- **The baya weaver** makes a beautiful nest of woven grass and leaves that it hangs from a tree or roof.

- **In the breeding season**, the male paradise whydah grows 28 cm long tail feathers – almost twice the length of its body – for display in flight.

- **Most weavers** have short, strong beaks that they use for feeding on seeds and insects.

- **The red bishop** mates with three or four females, who all nest in his territory.

- **The red-vented malimbe** (a weaver) feeds mainly on the husks of oil palm nuts.

> ★ STAR FACT ★
> As many as 500 pairs of red-billed queleas may nest together in one acacia tree.

Plovers and lapwings

- **The wrybill**, a New Zealand plover, has a unique beak that curves to the right. The bird sweeps its beak over sand to pick up insects.

- **If a predator** comes near a killdeer's nest, the bird moves away, trailing a wing to look as though it is injured. The predator, seeing what it thinks is an easy victim, follows the killdeer which, once far enough away, flies off.

- **Kentish plover chicks** have markings like the stones and pebbles of their nest site. If danger threatens, the chicks flatten themselves on the ground and are almost impossible to see.

▶ *The wrybill breeds on New Zealand's South Island, but overwinters on North Island.*

- **There are 60 or so species of plovers** and lapwings around the world.

- **Female dotterels** lay clutches of eggs for several males, which incubate the eggs.

- **To attract females**, the male lapwing performs a spectacular rolling, tumbling display flight in the air.

- **Spur-winged plovers** are often seen close to crocodiles in Africa and Asia – they may feed on small creatures that the crocodiles disturb.

- **The lapwing** is also known as the peewit.

- **Golden plovers** have been recorded flying at more than 113 km/h.

> ★ STAR FACT ★
> Many plovers pat the ground with their feet to imitate the sound of rain. This attracts worms to the surface, where they are snapped up.

Penguins

- **Not all of the 18 species of penguin** live in Antarctica. A few species live around Australia and South Africa, and there is even one resident in the Galapagos Islands on the equator.

- **Penguins have wings**, but cannot fly. They spend as much as 85% of their time in water, where they use their wings like flippers to help push themselves through the water.

- **The king penguin** has been known to dive down to 250 m in search of prey.

- **An emperor penguin** may travel at least 900 km

An emperor penguin stands about 110 cm high

◀ *An emperor chick spends the first 2 months of its life on its parent's feet, protected from the cold by a pouch of skin. If it falls off, it freezes to death in seconds.*

> ★ STAR FACT ★
> The male emperor penguin incubates his mate's eggs for 60 days, eating nothing and losing as much as 45% of his body weight.

on one feeding expedition.

- **Like many other penguins**, gentoos nest in a simple scrape on the ground, but they surround it with a ring of pebbles. A courting gentoo shows its mate an example of the sort of pebbles it will provide.

- **The emperor penguin** keeps its egg warm on its feet, where it is covered by a fold of skin. The temperature there stays at 36°C, despite the freezing surroundings.

- **Penguins** eat fish, squid and shellfish. They have spiny tongues to help them hold on to slippery prey.

- **A dense covering** of three layers of feathers keeps penguins warm. An emperor penguin has about 12 feathers per square cm of his body.

- **Penguins** usually swim at 5–10 km/h, but can reach speeds of up to 24 km/h.

Emperor penguin chick

▲ Emperor penguins are highly streamlined, allowing them to dive to depths of 500 m when they hunt. They can stay underwater for more than fifteen minutes, using their strong flippers to propel them forward.

Bird song and calls

- **Birds** make two sorts of sounds – simple calls, giving a warning or a threat, and the more complicated songs sung by some males at breeding time.

- **Birds' songs** have a definite dialect. The songs of a group of chaffinches in one area, will sound slightly different from those of a group somewhere else.

- **A songbird** reared in captivity away from its family produces a weak version of its parents' song, but cannot perform the whole repertoire.

- **Gulls and parrots** do not sing, but they do make various calls to attract mates or warn off enemies.

- **A bird sings** by vibrating the thin muscles in its syrinx – a special organ in its throat.

- **A sedge warbler** may use at least 50 different sounds in its songs.

- **Male and female boubou shrikes** sing a duet together, performing alternate parts of the song.

- **Songbirds** may make as many as 20 calls; gulls make only about 10.

- **Birds** make other sounds, too. During courtship flights, male woodpigeons make a loud clapping with their wings.

◀ The chaffinch is the commonest of Europe's finches.

> ★ **STAR FACT** ★
> A baby songbird starts to learn to sing about 10 days after it hatches, and continues to learn for about 40 days.

Shrikes and vangas

- **If it has plenty of prey**, such as lizards, frogs or insects, the northern shrike will store items for later by impaling them on a thorn bush or barbed wire fence.

- **Shrikes** are also known as 'butcher birds', because of their habit of hanging prey in trees.

- **The 14 species of vanga** live only on Madagascar and the neighbouring Comoros Islands.

- **The fiscal shrike** is an aggressive bird that kills other birds which come near it.

- **During its courtship display**, the male puffback (a shrike) fluffs up the long feathers on its lower back like a powder puff.

▲ The beautiful crimson-breasted shrike often uses strips of acacia bark to build its nest.

- **There are about 65 species of shrikes** found in Africa, Europe, Asia and North America, as well as 72 species of cuckoo-shrikes and 9 species of helmet shrikes.

- **All shrikes** have powerful hooked beaks that they use for killing insects, lizards and frogs.

- **The call of the brubru shrike** sounds just like a phone ring.

- **The loggerhead shrike** makes a nest of twigs and grass in a thorny bush or tree, where the female incubates 5–7 eggs.

- **The sickle-billed vanga** uses its long, curved beak to probe bark for insects. It hangs upside down by its claws while it feeds.

Tits

- **The blue tit** is only 10–11 cm long, but lays as many as 15 eggs – more than any other bird that feeds its young.

- **The largest of the tits** is the Asian sultan tit, at about 22 cm long and 30 g in weight – twice the size of most tits.

- **The penduline tit** makes an amazing nest woven from plant fibres and suspended from the end of a twig. The walls of the nest may be 2.5 cm thick.

- **There are about 50 species of true tits** found in Europe, Africa, Asia and North America. There are also 7 species of long-tailed tits and 10 species of penduline tits.

◀ *Agile little blue tits and their relatives can often be seen clinging to wire bird feeders in gardens during the winter.*

★ **STAR FACT** ★

The willow tit may bury up to 1000 nuts and seeds a day, to eat later when food is scarce.

- **The black-capped chickadee** gets its name from its call, which sounds like a 'chick-a-dee-dee', and is one of the most complex of any bird songs.

- **The female great tit** lays 8–13 eggs, each of which is about 10% of her body weight.

- **Great tits** hatch blind and helpless, and are fed by their parents for about 3 weeks. The parents may make 1000 feeding trips a day to the young.

- **The long-tailed tit** makes its nest from feathers and moss that it collects – one nest may contain as many as 2000 feathers in all.

- **The long-tailed tit** is only about 14 cm long, and more than half of its length is its tail feathers.

Pigeons and sandgrouse

- **The passenger pigeon** was once one of the most common birds in North America – one flock was 480 km long and 1.6 km wide. But overhunting made the birds rare, and the last passenger pigeon died in captivity in 1914.

- **Both male and female pigeons** can make a milky substance in their crops that they feed to their young.

- **Wood pigeons** feed on leaves, seeds, nuts, berries and some insects, but those living near humans also eat bread and food scraps.

- **At about 74 cm long** (nearly as big as a turkey), the Victoria crowned pigeon of New Guinea is the largest member of its family.

- **Pigeon 'races'** are held

▲ *Sandgrouse usually have grey or brownish feathers with mottled patterns that blend with their desert surroundings.*

in which birds return to their homes from 1000 km away.

- **The 16 or so species of sandgrouse** live in southern Europe, Africa and parts of Asia.

- **One adult sandgrouse** was found to have 8000 seeds in its crop.

★ **STAR FACT** ★

A male sandgrouse soaks his belly feathers at a desert waterhole, then flies back to his nest so the chicks can drink from his plumage.

- **In Christianity**, a dove is often used to symbolize the Holy Spirit. Doves are often released as a gesture of peace and goodwill.

- **There are more than 300 species of pigeon**, and they occur all over the world, except in the far north and Antarctica.

Hawks and harriers

- **The female sparrowhawk** is almost twice the size of the male. At breeding time she defends the nest while the more agile male brings the family food.

- **The marsh harrier** flies close to the ground searching for mice, rats, frogs, rabbits and even fish. When it sights prey, it swoops down, seizes the victim in its sharp talons and tears it apart with its beak.

- **Tiny spines** on the underside of the black-collared hawk's toes help it catch and hold slippery fish prey.

- **The African harrier hawk** likes to feed on baby birds. It has long, double-jointed legs that allow it to reach into other birds' nests and grab the chicks.

- **There are about 66** species of hawks and harriers, including goshawks and sparrowhawks.

- **Young goshawks** first leave the nest at about 40 days old and start to fly at about 45 days. By 50 days or so they can hunt for themselves, and by 70 days they can manage without their parents.

- **The largest hawk** is the northern goshawk, which is up to 60 cm long and weighs as much as 1.3 kg.

- **Fledgling goshawks** 'play' as a way of practising their hunting skills.

- **At least 95%** of the northern harrier's diet is mice.

- **The smallest hawk** is the African little sparrowhawk, which is only about 25 cm long.

◀ *The sparrowhawk preys mostly on other birds, ranging in size from tits to pheasants.*

Rails and bustards

▼ *The great bustard, with its 2.5 m wingspan, lives on the plains, steppes and farmland of Europe and Asia, feeding mainly on insects.*

- **The weka** is a flightless rail that lives in New Zealand. Its diet includes seeds, fruit, mice, eggs and insects, and it also scavenges in rubbish bins.

- **Female great bustards** are much smaller and lighter than males, weighing only about 5 kg.

- **The world's smallest flightless bird**, the Inaccessible Island rail, weighs only 35 g – about the same as a small tomato. It lives on Inaccessible Island in the South Atlantic Ocean.

- **There are more than 130 species of rails** found all over the world, including many small islands. The family includes moorhens, coots and crakes, as well as rails.

- **The takahe**, a large flightless rail, is now extremely rare and lives only in South Island, New Zealand.

- **The 22 species of bustard** live in Africa, southern Europe, Asia and Australia.

- **Fights between Asian watercocks** (a type of rail) are staged for sport in some parts of Asia.

- **Coots** are the most aquatic of all the rails. They dive in search of plants and water insects to eat.

- **The female moorhen** makes a nest of dead leaves at the water's edge. The male helps incubate the 5–11 eggs.

> ★ STAR FACT ★
> The great bustard of southern Europe and Asia is the world's heaviest flying bird. The male weighs up to 18 kg.

Prehistoric birds

- **The earliest known bird** is *Archaeopteryx*, which lived 155 million years ago. It had feathers like a modern bird but teeth like a reptile.

- *Ichthyornis* was a seabird with long, toothed jaws. It lived alongside dinosaurs in the Late Cretaceous period.

- **Although it could fly,** *Archaeopteryx* could not take off from the ground, and probably had to climb a tree before launching itself into the air.

- **Scientists believe** that birds evolved from lightly built dinosaurs such as *Compsognathus*, which ran on two legs.

◀ *Archaeopteryx had a wingspan of about 50 cm. Its name means 'ancient wing'.*

- **The dodo** stood 1 m tall and lived on the island of Mauritius. It became extinct in the 17th century.

- *Aepyornis*, a 3-m tall ostrich ancestor from Madagascar, probably became extinct in the 17th century.

- **The eggs** of Aepyornis, or elephant bird may have weighed as much as 10 kg – more than 9 times the weight of an ostrich egg today.

- **The tallest bird ever** was the moa (Dinornis) of New Zealand. It was a towering 3.5 m tall.

- **The great auk** first lived 2 million years ago. It became extinct in the mid 19th century after being overhunted for its fat, which was burned in oil lamps.

- **An early member** of the vulture family, *Argentavix* of South America had an amazing 7.3 m wingspan.

Waxwings and relatives

- **The waxwing** gets its name from the red markings like drops of wax at the tips of its wing feathers.

- **Palmchats** nest in palm trees. One nest may house 30 pairs of birds, each with its own tunnel entrance to the outside.

- **The silky flycatcher** feeds mostly on mistletoe berries, passing out the seeds.

Prominent crest

◀ *Bohemian waxwings will strip a bush clean of its berries before moving on.*

> ★ STAR FACT ★
> When courting, a male bohemian waxwing gives the female a gift – a berry or ant larva.

- **The bohemian waxwing** makes a nest of twigs, moss and grass, usually in a conifer tree. The female incubates 4–6 eggs, while the male keeps her fed.

- **Adult cedar waxwings** store berries in their crops, or throat pouches, and regurgitate them for their young.

- **The male silky flycatcher** builds a nest for his mate's eggs, and does most of the incubation.

- **Adult waxwings** eat mainly berries, but feed their young on insects for the first two weeks of their lives.

- **The single species of palmchat** is found on the islands of Haiti and the Dominican Republic in the Caribbean.

- **Cedar waxwings** have been seen sitting in rows on a branch passing a berry from one bird to the next until one of them swallows it!

True and harpy eagles

- **The most powerful of all eagles**, the South American harpy eagle hunts prey that may weigh more than itself, such as large monkeys and sloths.

- **The Philippine eagle** is one of the rarest of all birds of prey. Twenty years ago there were only about 200 birds. Now they are strictly protected, and there is a captive breeding programme to increase numbers.

- **The golden eagle** makes a bulky nest of sticks and branches that may measure as much as 2 m high and 1.5 m across often called the eyrie.

- **A harpy eagle** weighs over 8 kg, has a wingspan of more than 2 m, and talons the size of a bear's claws.

- **True eagles** are also known as booted eagles, because their legs are covered with feathers down to their toes.

- **Verreaux's eagle** lays 2 eggs, but the first chick to hatch usually kills the younger chick.

- **At up to 96 cm long**, the martial eagle is the largest African eagle. It feeds on mammals such as hyrax and young antelope, and on other

> **★ STAR FACT ★**
> A eaglet weighs only 85 g when it hatches, but by the time it reaches adulthood the bird weighs about 7 kg.

birds, including guineafowl and even storks.

- **A young martial eagle** is fed by its parents for about 60 days, by which time is has a full covering of feathers and is able to tear up prey for itself.

- **The golden eagle** usually has a hunting territory of about 260 sq km.

Hooked beak for tearing apart its prey

Large eyes – the eagle has excellent eyesight

Tapering wing feathers increase lift so the eagle can soar for long periods

Long curved talons

▶ Golden eagles lay 2 eggs, but one chick usually dies. At first the mother keeps the surviving chick warm while the male finds food, but as the chick grows larger, both parents are kept busy supplying it with food.

Turkeys and grouse

- **Male wild turkeys** of the USA, Mexico and Central America can weigh up to 8 kg.

- **At 87 cm long**, the western capercaillie is the biggest of the 17 species of grouse. The female is only 60 cm long.

▲ *Wild turkeys usually feed on the ground, but they are strong flyers over short distances.*

- **In winter**, the spruce grouse feeds mainly on the buds and needles of pine trees.

- **An adult turkey** has about 3500 feathers.

- **The 17 species of grouse** live in North America, Europe and northern Asia.

- **Wild turkeys** are not fussy eaters. They feed on seeds, nuts, berries, leaves, insects and other small creatures.

- **To attract females** and challenge rival males, the ruffed grouse makes a drumming sound with its wings.

- **At the start of the breeding season**, foot-stamping dances are performed by groups of male prairie chickens at their traditional display areas.

- **The ruffed grouse** lays 9–12 eggs. When the young hatch, the female shows them where to find food.

Mockingbirds and relatives

- **Mockingbirds** are so-called because they imitate the calls of other bird species – as many as 36 in all.

- **The alpine accentor** breeds high in the mountains, and has been seen nesting at 8000 m in the Himalayas.

- **As well as mockingbirds,** the 32 species in the family includes birds such as catbirds, thrashers and tremblers. The live in North and South America.

- **The brown trembler**, a resident of some Caribbean islands, gets its name from its habit of shaking its body from time to time.

- **The 13 accentor species** live in mountainous parts of northern Africa, Europe and Asia.

▶ *The northern mockingbird is the best mimic in its family, usually copying the sounds made by other bird species.*

- **'Mimic of many tongues'** is the meaning of the northern mockingbird's scientific name, *Mimus polyglottus*.

- **The grey catbird** lines its cup-shaped nest of sticks, leaves and grasses with pine needles and even hair. The female lays 3–5 eggs, and incubates them for 12–13 days.

- **The brown thrasher** scatters dead leaves with its beak as it searches on the ground for its insect prey.

- **The catbird** gets its name from its strange, catlike call.

Wrens and babblers

- **The white-necked rockfowl** (babbler family) makes a mud nest on the roof of caves. It sometimes builds onto old wasps' nests.

- **The cactus wren** builds its nest among the spines of the chola cactus. Few enemies will brave the spines to steal the wren's eggs or young.

- **At about 23 cm long**, the black-capped donacobious of South America is the largest of the wren family.

- **The only species** of the babbler family to live in North America is the wren-tit, while 256 species are found in Asia, Africa and Australasia.

- **The tuneful song** of the red-billed leiothrix (babbler family) makes it a popular cage bird in China.

- **Although common in west Africa**, the pale-breasted thrush-babbler is so good at hiding on the forest floor, where it searches for insects, that it is rarely seen.

- **A male wren** courts a mate by building up to 12 nests. The female chooses one in which to lay her eggs.

▶ The cactus wren makes several decoy nests in different cactus plants to fool predators.

- **The winter wren** usually lays 5–8 eggs, and incubates them for 14–17 days. The young stay in the nest for 20 days.

- **Brightly coloured patches** of bare skin on the head are a distinguishing feature of rockfowl (babbler family).

- **Most wrens** live in Europe, Asia, Africa and North America.

Caring for young

- **Many baby birds** are blind, naked and helpless when they hatch, and have to be cared for by their parents.

- **The young of ducks and geese** hatch with a covering of feathers, and can find food hours after hatching.

- **A young golden eagle** has grown feathers after 50 days and learned to fly after 70, but stays with its parents for another month while learning to hunt.

★ STAR FACT ★
In a colony of thousands of terns, baby terns can recognize the call of their own parents.

- **A young bird** is known as a fledgling from the time it hatches until it is fully feathered and can fly.

- **A young pelican** feeds by putting its head deep into its parent's large beak and gobbling up any fish it finds.

- **A swan** carries its young on its back to keep them safe.

- **To obtain food** from its parent, a young herring gull has to peck at a red spot on the parent's beak. The adult gull then regurgitates food for the chick to eat.

- **Shearwaters** feed their young for 60 days, then stop. After a week the chicks get so hungry that they take to the air to find food for themselves.

- **In 3 weeks**, a new-born cuckoo gets 50 times heavier.

◀ Bokmakierie shrike chicks are born blind, but can see by 4 days old.

Ostriches and emus

- **The ostrich** is the largest of all birds alive today. It stands 2.5 m tall and weighs about 130 kg – more than twice as much as an average human.

- **The male emu** incubates his mate's clutch of eggs for 8 weeks, during which time he does not eat or drink. He lives on the stores of body fat that it has built up during the previous months.

- **In Southwest Asia**, the shells of ostrich eggs are believed to have magical powers, and are sometimes placed on the roofs of houses as protection from evil.

- **Ostriches don't really bury their heads** in the sand. But if a female is approached by an enemy while sitting on her nest on the ground, she will press her long neck flat on the ground, to appear less obvious.

- **The largest bird in Australia** is the emu, which measures 2 m tall and weighs as much as 45 kg. Like the ostrich, it cannot fly.

> ★ STAR FACT ★
> The ostrich cannot fly, but is a very fast runner. It can speed along at 60 km/h – as fast as a racehorse.

- **An ostrich feather** was used as a symbol of justice in ancient Egypt.

- **Seeds, fruits, flowers and plant shoots** are the emu's main sources of food, but it also eats some insects and small animals.

- **The male ostrich** makes a shallow nest on the ground and mates with several females, all of whom lay their eggs in the nest. The chief female incubates the eggs during the day, and the male takes over at night.

- **Ostrich chicks** have many enemies, including jackals and hyenas, and only 15% are likely to survive until their first birthday.

The male has black feathers on its back; females and young birds have brown feathers

The long, flexible neck is bare skinned

Long, strong legs for running

▲ The ostrich lives in Africa in dry grassland areas, where it often has to run for long distances in search of food.

Migration

- **Migration** is generally the journey made twice a year between a summer breeding area, where food is plentiful, and a wintering area with a good climate.

- **Many migrating birds** have to build up fat stores to allow them to fly non-stop for many days without food.

- **A migrating bird** can fly across the Sahara Desert in 50–60 hours without stopping to 'refuel'.

- **Birds find their way** by observing landmarks, the patterns of stars and the position of the setting sun. They also use their sense of smell and monitor the Earth's magnetic field.

- **Most birds** that migrate long distances fly at night.

- **The snow goose** migrates nearly 5000 km south from Arctic Canada at an altitude of 9000 m.

- **Before migration was studied**, some people thought swallows simply spent the winter asleep in mud.

- **Even flightless birds migrate.** Emus make journeys on foot of 500 km or more, and penguins migrate in water.

- **Every year** at least 5 billion birds migrate from North to Central and South America.

- **The Arctic tern** spends the northern summer in the Arctic and migrates to the Antarctic for the southern summer, enjoying 24 hours of daylight in both places.

▼ *Geese migrate in huge flocks, but pairs stay together within the flock.*

Finches and relatives

- **The crossbill** gets its name from its crossed beak, specially shaped for extracting seeds from pine cones.

- **The beaks** of some crossbills cross to the left, while those of others cross to the right.

- **Canaries** were first domesticated in the early 16th century, from the island canary of the Canary Islands, the Azores and Madeira.

- **The male American goldfinch** brings the female food while she incubates the 4–6 eggs.

- **The bullfinch** feeds on fruit buds in spring and it can pluck as many as 30 buds in a minute.

- **The kernels** of cherry stones and olive stones are a favourite food of the strong-beaked hawfinch.

- **The goldfinch** uses its slender beak like tweezers to take seeds from between the spines of a teasel head.

- **Finches are small birds**, ranging from 4-19 cm long and weighing up to 100 grams.

- **Siskins and goldfinches** have long been popular as cage birds, and are now rare in many areas.

▲ *Wild canaries have duller plumage than their bright yellow domestic relatives.*

★ STAR FACT ★
Although the hawfinch weighs only 50 g, its beak can exert a pressure of 45 kg.

Cranes and trumpeters

- **The whooping crane** is one of the world's most endangered birds, with only about 300 surviving in 1995.

- **The crowned crane**, which has a fine crest of yellow feathers, performs a spectacular courtship display that involves leaping 2 m into the air.

- **The 3 species of trumpeter** live in tropical rainforests. All make a loud trumpeting call – hence their name.

- **In China and Japan** the crane symbolizes long life and good luck.

- **At about 1.5 m long**, the Sarus crane of India, Southeast Asia and northern Australia is one of the largest members of the crane family.

▶ *The handsome crowned crane lives in Africa, usually around swamps and marshland.*

- **The limpkin** is a relative of the cranes and the only member of its family. It has a long, curved beak, which it uses to remove snails from their shells.

- **Trumpeters** spend most of their time on the ground in search of fruit, nuts and insects, but they roost in trees.

- **The sandhill crane** makes a nest of plant material on the ground. The female lays 2 eggs, which both parents help to incubate. Soon after hatching, the young leave the nest.

- **Siberian cranes** have been known to live more than 80 years – one captive male even fathered chicks at the age of 78!

- **The 14 or so species of crane** live all over the world, in North America, Africa, Europe, Asia and Australia.

Bowerbirds

- **Male bowerbirds** build bowers of twigs and other plant material to attract females. They decorate their creations with berries and shells, and some perform dances in front of their bowers.

- **The Vogelkop gardener bowerbird** builds a hutlike structure big enough for a person to crawl into.

- **Male bowerbirds' bowers** are not built as a place for the

◀ *The male spotted bowerbird spends much of its time looking after its bower.*

female to lay eggs and rear young. The females build their own, more practical nests.

- **The forests** of New Guinea and northern and eastern Australia are home to the 18 or so species of bowerbird.

- **At about 36 cm long**, the great grey bowerbird of northern Australia is the largest of the family.

- **Bowerbirds** feed on fruit, berries, seeds, insects and other small creatures.

- **A female bowerbird** cares for her 1–3 chicks alone.

- **The male regent bowerbird** paints its bower yellow using a mix of spit and the juice of crushed leaves.

- **Catbirds** are members of the bowerbird family. They get their name from their catlike calls.

Feathers

- **Feathers** are made of a protein called keratin. Human hair and nails are also made of keratin.

- **Feathers grow** at a rate of 1–13 mm a day.

- **The ruby-throated hummingbird** has only 940 feathers, while the whistling swan has 25,216.

▲ The peacock has the most ornate feathers of any bird.

- **A bird's feathers** are replaced once or twice a year in a process called 'moulting'.

- **Feathers** keep a bird warm, protect its skin, provide camouflage, and may also attract mates.

- **In most birds**, a third of the feathers are on the head.

- **The longest feathers ever known** were 10.59 m long, and belonged to an ornamental chicken.

- **The feathers** that cover a bird's body are called contour feathers. Down feathers underneath provide extra warmth.

- **The 7182 feathers** of a bald eagle weighed 677 g, more than twice as much as the bird's skeleton.

- **Birds** spend time every day 'preening' – cleaning and rearranging their feathers with their beaks.

▶ The plumage of the little hummingbird gleams with iridescence.

Antbirds and tapaculos

- **Antbirds** follow columns of army ants as they march over the forest floor, perching just above the ground to seize other insects as they flee from the ants.

- **The 230 or so species of antbird** live in Mexico, Central and South America.

- **The 30 species of tapaculos** are insect-eating birds that live in dry scrub and the cool mountain forests of South America.

- **Antbirds** mate for life.

- **During the courtship ritual** of the ocellated antbird, the male presents the female with an item of food.

- **Antbirds have white spots** on their back feathers, which they use to signal

> ★ STAR FACT ★
> An antbird rubs a mouthful of ants over its feathers to clean them. The formic acid from the ants kills any lice and mites in the feathers.

warnings to each other. They show the spots in particular patterns according to the message – like a sort of Morse code.

- **Antbird species** range from 10–38 cm long, and have differently shaped beaks to suit their food.

- **Some larger species of antbirds** have a special 'tooth' inside the beak that helps them chew food.

- **Most antbirds** do not fly much and have poorly developed wings, but their legs are strong, for running and perching.

◀ Female antbirds are often brownish or greenish in colour. Males usually have dark grey plumage with white markings.

Swallows and martins

- **There are about 80 species of swallows and martins** found all over the world. Most migrate between breeding grounds and wintering areas.

- **The sand martin** digs a 120 cm long nesting burrow in river banks.

- **Swallows** catch their insect food in the air as they fly.

- **Only discovered in 1968,** the white-eyed river martin spends the winter in reedbeds on Lake Boraphet in Thailand.

- **Purple martins** often nest in old woodpecker holes or in nest-boxes. The female incubates the 4–5 eggs

> ★ STAR FACT ★
> The ancient Romans used swallows as messengers to carry news of the winners of chariot races to neighbouring towns.

▼ *The house martin often lives near people, making its nest under the eaves of buildings or under bridges or other structures.*

alone, but the male helps feed the young.

- **There is an old saying** that the weather will be good when swallows fly high, but bad when swallows fly low. This is based on fact – in wet weather, insects tend to stay nearer the ground, so their predators – the swallows – do the same.

- **Adult swallows** will carry a mass of crushed insects, squashed in a ball in the throat, back to their young. A barn swallow may take 400 meals a day to its chicks.

- **Sand martins** breed in the northern hemisphere, migrating south in the winter in flocks of thousands.

- **In most swallow species** males and females are alike, but in the rare blue swallow the female has a short tail, while the male's is long and forked.

Snake and sea eagles

- **The bald eagle** performs an amazing courtship display, in which male and female lock their claws together and tumble through the air towards the ground.

- **The short-toed eagle** kills a snake with a bite to the back of the head, instantly severing the backbone.

- **The white-tailed sea eagle** snatches fish from the water in its powerful talons.

- **The bald eagle** was chosen as the national emblem of the USA in 1782, and appears on most of the gold and silver coins in the USA.

- **Spikes** on the underside of its toes help the African fish eagle hold

onto its fish prey. It also catches birds, terrapins and baby crocodiles.

- **Bald eagles** are not really bald. They have white feathers on their heads, which may make them appear bald from a distance.

- **The bateleur**, a snake eagle, may fly as much as 300 km a day in search of food.

- **Snake eagles** do eat snakes, and have short, strong toes ideal for tackling their writhing victims.

- **The name 'bateleur'** means 'tumbler' or 'tightrope walker' in French, and refers to the rocking, acrobatic movements that the bird makes in flight.

- **There are only about 40 pairs** of the Madagascar fish eagle left in the world.

◀ *Steller's sea eagle lives along Asia's coasts and rivers, preying mostly on salmon.*

Rainforest birds

- **Male and female eclectus parrots** of the Amazon rainforest have very different plumage. The male bird is mostly bright green, while the female is red with a blue underside.

- **The crowned eagle** lives in African rainforests, where it feeds on monkeys and other mammals such as mongooses and rats.

- **The king vulture** of South America is the only vulture to live in rainforest. As well as feeding on carrion, it also kills mammals and reptiles.

- **The sunbittern** lives along river banks in the rainforests of South America, feeding on frogs, insects and other creatures.

- **With its abundance** of flowers, leaves, fruits and insects all year round, a rainforest is the ideal home for many different kinds of birds.

- **The muscovy duck**, now familiar in farmyards and parks in many parts of the world, originally came from the rainforests of Central and South America.

- **Large, flightless cassowaries** live in the rainforests of New Guinea, where people hunt them to eat.

- **The spectacled eagle owl** of South America has rings of white feathers around its eyes. Its call resembles the hammering sound made by woodpeckers.

- **The rare Cassin's hawk eagle** lives in African rainforests, and hunts squirrels and other birds.

★ STAR FACT ★
The hoatzin builds its nest over rainforest rivers, so that if its chicks are threatened, they can drop into the water to escape.

Huge eagles nest at the tops of the highest rainforest trees

Macaws, parrots, toucans and many other species flutter through the rainforest canopy

The stunning, resplendent quetzal favours trees of the laurel family

▶ The tropical rainforest has more types of bird than anywhere else. Many of the birds in the canopy are amazingly colourful. Game birds and little insect eaters patrol the forest floor.

Larks and wagtails

- **The shore lark** has the widest distribution of any lark. Its habitats range from the icy Arctic to deserts.

- **The wagtail family** has about 60 species, most of which are small, insect-eating birds. They include pipits and longclaws.

- **The 75 species of lark** live in North America, parts of South America, Africa, Europe, Asia and Australia. The greatest number of species is found in Africa.

- **The female skylark** makes a shallow, grassy nest on the ground, and incubates 3–4 eggs.

- **The skylark** performs a beautiful song as it flutters up to a great height, hovers and descends again.

- **The thick-billed lark** has a larger, stronger beak than most larks, and uses it to crush hard seeds and tough-shelled insects.

- **The shore or horned lark** is the only member of the family to live in the Americas.

- **The desert lark's coloration** varies according to where it lives – birds in areas of white sand have pale feathers, while those that live on dark laval sand are almost black.

- **Craneflies** are one of the favourite foods of the meadow pipit. Adults may feed their 3–5 chicks on craneflies for 2 weeks. The chicks develop in a nest of dry grass lined with hair.

★ **STAR FACT** ★
The yellow-throated longclaw gets its name from the 5-cm long claw on each back toe.

◀ *The little pied wagtail bobs its tail up and down almost all the time as it searches for insects.*

Kingfishers

- **The common kingfisher** nests at the end of a 60-cm long tunnel that it excavates in a river bank. The female lays 4–8 eggs.

- **The tiny African pygmy kingfisher** dives not into water, like the common kingfisher, but into grass, where it snatches grasshoppers and beetles.

- **The 86 or so species of kingfisher** are found all over the world, except parts of the far north.

- **The giant kingfisher** of Africa and the Australian laughing kookaburra are the largest of the family, at about 45 cm long.

- **Common kingfishers** incubate their eggs for 19–21 days, and feed the young for up to 4 weeks.

- **The shovel-billed kingfisher** is armed with its own spade for digging in mud – it uses its large, heavy bill to dig up worms, shellfish and small reptiles.

- **A flash of iridescent turquoise feathers** streaking at high speed along a river bank indicates the presence of a common or European kingfisher.

- **In the forests of New Guinea**, the male paradise kingfisher shows off its very long tail feathers to females as part of its courtship display.

- **The laughing kookaburra** is named for its call, which sounds like noisy laughter. It makes its call to claim territory. Once one starts, others tend to join in!

- **In northern Australia**, termite mounds are adopted as nest sites by the buff-breasted kingfisher.

◀ *The kingfisher fiercely defends the stretch of river bank where it feeds and nests.*

Thrushes and dippers

- **The wheatear** breeds in the Arctic, but in autumn flies some 3200 km to Africa, where it spends the winter.

- **The dipper** is the only type of songbird to live in and around water – it can swim underwater and even walk along streambeds as it searches for insect prey.

- **The familiar orange-red breast** of a robin indicates that the bird is at least 2 months old.

- **More than 300 species of thrush** are found nearly all over the world.

- **Best known for its beautiful song**, the nightingale sings during the day as well as at night.

- **The female blackbird** makes a cup-shaped nest of plant stems, grass, twigs and roots. The 4–5 eggs hatch after 11–17 days.

- **The 5 species of dipper** live in Europe, Asia and parts of North and South America.

- **The dome-shaped nests** of dippers usually have an entrance over running water.

- **The American robin** – the largest of the North American thrushes – lives both in cities and mountains.

- **Blackbirds** were taken to Australia and New Zealand in the 19th century, and their songs are now clearly different to blackbirds living in Europe.

◀ *The European robin is Britain's national bird.*

Sandpipers

- **Coasts and marshes** are the home of the 88 or so species of sandpiper, which include curlews, snipe and phalaropes. Most have long beaks and long legs.

- **The western curlew** plunges its long, curved beak into soft coastal mud to find worms and clams.

- **As it dives towards Earth**, air rushing through the outermost tail feathers of the European snipe makes a sound called 'drumming'.

◀ *The curlew's long legs are ideal for wading through marshland.*

- **Sandpipers** range in size from the eastern curlew, at about 66 cm long, to the least sandpiper, at 11 cm.

- **Once the dowitcher's 4 eggs** have hatched, feeding the chicks is the sole responsibility of the male.

- **Unusually for birds**, female phalaropes are more brightly coloured than males. The female lays several clutches of eggs, leaving the male parent of each clutch to do all the caring for the young.

- **The turnstone** is so-named because it turns over stones on the beach in search of shellfish and worms.

- **In the breeding season**, male ruffs grow amazing feathers around the head and neck, and dance In groups to attract females.

> ★ STAR FACT ★
> The eskimo curlew is one of the world's rarest birds. With only 50 or so birds left in the world, it is on the brink of extinction.

Large seabirds

- **The wandering albatross** has the longest wings of any bird – from tip to tip they are an incredible 3.4 m.

- **The white-tailed tropicbird** is noted for its amazing tail streamers, which measure up to 40 cm long.

- **The male frigatebird** has a bright red throat pouch that he inflates during courtship to attract females.

- **The wandering albatross** often flies 500 km in a day, soaring over the ocean in search of food.

- **The pirates of the bird world** are frigatebirds, which often chase other seabirds in the air and harass them into giving up their catches.

- **Frigatebird chicks** depend on their parents for longer than most birds. They start to fly at about 6 months, but continue to be fed until they are 1 year old.

- **The 5 species of frigatebird** fly over tropical areas of all oceans. They spend most of their lives in the air, rarely descending to land on water.

- **The 3 species of tropicbird** are all expert in the air and can dive into the sea to find prey, but cannot walk on land. With their legs set far back on their bodies, they can only drag themselves along.

- **The wandering albatross** can only breed every other year. It incubates its eggs for 11 weeks, and the chicks do not fly until they are about 40 weeks old.

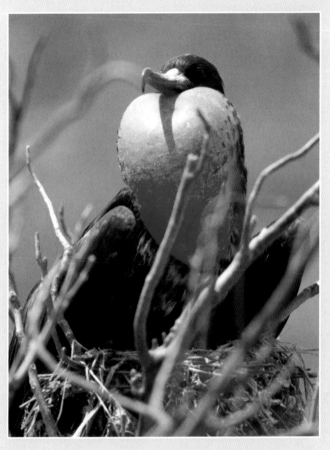

▲ When courting a mate, the male frigatebird clatters his beak and flaps his wings, as well as inflating his red throat pouch into an eyecatching balloon. Also known as a 'man of war', the frigatebird is adept at stealing food and nest material from other birds in the colony. It builds its large nest in trees.

> ★ STAR FACT ★
> A wandering albatross chick may eat as much as 100 kg of food during the time it is being fed by its parents.

Long wings for gliding on the wind

▶ Squid is the main food of the wandering albatross, but it will also snatch fish waste thrown from fishing boats. An expert glider, it can sail downwind from a height of about 15 m to just above the water's surface, before turning back into the wind to be blown upwards.

Sunbirds and relatives

- **The 115 or so species of sunbirds** live in tropical parts of Africa, Asia and Australia.

- **The Kauai o-o**, a honeyeater, was thought to be extinct, but in 1960 some birds were found, and there is now a very small protected population.

- **The flowerpecker family** contains about 58 species living in parts of Asia, Southeast Asia and Australia.

- **At about 23 cm long**, the Sao Tomé giant sunbird is the largest of its family. It uses its hooked beak to dig into the bark of trees for insects.

- **Sunbirds** use their long, slender beaks and tubular tongues to extract sweet liquid nectar from flowers.

- **Female sunbirds** make purse-shaped nests for their 2–3 eggs, which hatch after 13–15 days.

- **Honeyeaters** are the most important flower pollinators in Australia. The brushlike tip on the honeyeater's tongue helps it to extract flower nectar.

- **The crested berrypecker** (flowerpecker family) has a habit of rubbing its plumage with crushed flower petals.

- **The tui** (honeyeater family) of New Zealand is also known as the parson bird, because of the bib of white feathers at its throat.

▶ *Sunbirds feed from tropical flowers. They often hover as they do so, but cannot fly backwards like hummingbirds.*

> ★ **STAR FACT** ★
> The mistletoe bird (flowerpecker family) swallows mistletoe berries whole, digesting only the flesh and not the seeds.

Nests

- **The bald eagle** makes the biggest nest of any bird. It can be as large as 2.5 m across and 3.5 m deep – big enough for several people to hide inside!

- **The bee hummingbird's nest** is the smallest – only the size of a thimble.

- **The hammerkop**, a heronlike bird, makes a huge nest up to 2 m high and weighing 50 kg.

- **The hammerkop uses anything** from sticks to bits of bone and plastic to make its nest.

- **A cliff swallow's** nest is made up of about 1200 tiny balls of mud.

- **Nightjars** do not make a nest – they just lay their eggs on the ground.

- **The rufous-breasted castle builder** (woodcreeper family) makes a nest shaped like a dumb-bell, with two chambers – one for the chicks.

- **The turquoise-browed motmot** is a surprisingly efficient digger, excavating a 1.5-m long burrow in just 5 days.

- **The European bee-eater** nests underground to keep cool. While the surface temperature may reach 50°C, the bee-eater's nest remains a pleasant 25°C.

- **Hummingbirds and honeyeaters** use spiders' webs to hold their nests together.

▼ *A bald eagle's nest is used and enlarged year after year.*

Old World flycatchers

- **The spotted flycatcher** sits on a branch watching for insect prey, then darts out to catch it in mid-air – it has been seen catching 1 insect every 18 seconds.

- **The rufous-bellied niltava** lives and breeds in the Himalayas at altitudes of up to 2300 m.

- **The male pied flycatcher** may have two nests some distance apart, but he only helps rear the young in one of them.

- **There are 147 species of Old World flycatchers.** Some live in wooded parts of Europe, but they are more common in Asia, Africa and Australasia.

- **After a summer in Europe**, the red-breasted flycatcher flies to India and Southeast Asia for the winter.

- **The white-throated jungle flycatcher** is now very rare and lives only on two islands in the Philippines.

- **The female red-breasted flycatcher** makes a cup-shaped nest of moss, leaves, spiders' webs and plant down in which to lay her 5–6 eggs.

- **Male spotted flycatchers** bring all the food for their brood when they first hatch. Later, both parents feed the chicks.

- **Instead of catching all its food in the air**, the Australian flame robin often pounces onto its prey from a low perch.

- **In autumn and winter**, the pied flycatcher eats worms and berries as well as insects.

◄ *The spotted flycatcher lives in woodland, parks and gardens in Europe and parts of Asia and Africa.*

Ovenbirds and relatives

- **The nest** of the firewood-gatherer (ovenbird family) looks like a bonfire. A group of birds make the nest together and sleep in it during the winter.

- **The red-billed scythebill** (a woodcreeper) has a long, curved beak for delving deep into rainforest plants such as ferns and bromeliads to find insects.

- **Ovenbirds** live in the forests, mountains and semideserts of Mexico, Central and South America.

- **Woodcreepers** often nest in old woodpecker nests.

- **The common miner** (an ovenbird) digs a 3-m long burrow with a nest chamber at the end, where it raises its chicks and roosts for the rest of the year.

> ★ STAR FACT ★
> The rufous hornero's mud-and-straw nest is shaped like an old-fashioned clay oven.

- **Des Murs' wiretail** (an ovenbird) has only 6 tail feathers, 4 of which may be 3 times the length of the body.

- **The 50 or so species of woodcreeper** live in forests and woodland in Mexico, Central and South America.

- **Insects and spiders** hiding among the densely packed leaves of bromeliads may be extracted by the long, probing beak of the long-billed woodcreeper.

- **The campo miner** (an ovenbird) nests in a very particular place – an old armadillo burrow.

◄ *The rufous hornero is the national bird of Argentina.*

Polar and tundra birds

- **The willow ptarmigan** lives on the Arctic tundra. In winter it has white feathers that help to keep it hidden in the snow, but in summer it grows darker feathers again.

- **The ivory gull** of Arctic coasts and islands is the only all-white gull.

- **Adelie penguins** breed on coasts and islands around the Antarctic in huge colonies that return to the same site year after year.

- **Snowy owls** are among the fiercest Arctic birds. They soar over the tundra preying on other birds and small mammals such as lemmings.

- **Most birds leave Antarctica in winter**, but the southern black-backed gull stays all year round, feeding on fish, birds' eggs and carrion.

- **The emperor penguin** breeds in colder temperatures than any other bird. It survives temperatures of -40°C as it incubates its egg.

▲ In winter, the willow ptarmigan feeds mainly on the twigs and buds of dwarf willows.

- **The great skua** is the biggest flying bird in Antarctica, at up to 5 kg and 66 cm long.

- **Although only 10 cm long**, the little storm petrel may migrate 40,000 km a year between the poles.

- **The laysan albatross** breeds on central Pacific islands, but spends most of the year flying over the Arctic hunting for schools of fish to eat.

- **Tufted puffins** nest only on cliffs and islands in the Arctic North Pacific. One colony contained as many as 1 million nests.

Avocets and relatives

- **Young jacanas** often hide underneath floating leaves if danger threatens.

- **The 7 species of stilts and avocets** are all long-legged wading birds with long, slender beaks.

- **Female pheasant-tailed jacanas** mate with up to 10 males in one breeding season. The males incubate the eggs and care for the young.

- **If a male pheasant-tailed jacana** thinks his eggs are in danger, he may move them one at a time, holding them between its breast and throat.

- **The long, curved**

> ★ STAR FACT ★
> The American jacana or lilytrotter has extremely long toes and claws allowing it to walk on floating waterlily leaves.

beak of the pied avocet turns up at the end. The bird sweeps this strange tool through mud or shallow water to find worms and shrimps.

- **The black-winged stilt** has extremely long, bright pink legs that allow it to wade in deeper water than other stilts as it searches for worms and shellfish.

- **Jacanas** range in size from 16–53 cm long.

- **Avocets** nest in a hollow in the ground, lined with dead leaves. Both partners incubate the 3–5 eggs.

- **Young avocets** can run soon after hatching, and can fend for themselves after 6 weeks.

◀ The African jacana is common around lakes and marshes, where it feeds on insects, fish and water plants.

Lyrebirds and relatives

- **One of the biggest of all the songbirds**, the superb lyrebird has an extraordinary lyre-shaped tail, with feathers more than 50 cm long.

- **The rifleman**, one of the 3 species of New Zealand wren, lays eggs that are about 20% of her body weight. She and the male recruit helpers to bring food to their young.

- **The 2 species of scrub-bird** live in Australia, where they feed on insects, lizards and frogs.

- **In its loud song**, the lyrebird may imitate other birds, barking dogs, chainsaws and even passing trains.

- **The female lyrebird** builds a domed nest, usually close to the ground. Her 1 chick stays with her for 8 months or more.

- **The rufous scrub-bird** spends most of its time on the and rarely flies.

◀ *The lyrebird spends most of its life on the ground searching for insects.*

- **The 2 species of lyrebird** live in dense mountain forest in southeastern Australia.

- **Named after the small island** in Cook Strait where it lived, the Stephen Island wren was killed off by the lighthouse keeper's cat. It may have been the only flightless songbird.

- **A full-grown rufous scrub-bird** is 16–18 cm long and weighs about 30 g.

- **Young male superb lyrebirds** do not grow their lyre-shaped tails until they are 3 or 4 years old.

Eggs

- **All bird species** lay eggs.

- **The biggest egg** is the ostrich egg. At 1.5 kg, it is 30 times heavier than an average hen's egg.

- **Incubation** is the process of keeping eggs warm while they develop. It can take from 10–80 days.

- **The yellow yolk** in an egg provides food for the growing embryo. The white provides food and moisture.

- **Gannets stand on their eggs** to keep them warm!

- **The shell of an egg** contains 50–100 tiny pores per sq cm, allowing oxygen to seep into the egg and carbon dioxide does the same outwards

- **Egg yolks** are not always yellow. The common tern's yolk is deep red, and the gentoo penguin's a pinky red.

> **★ STAR FACT ★**
> The bee hummingbird lays the smallest egg, at just 0.3 g. You could fit 4700 into 1 ostrich egg!

- **Eggshells** vary in thickness from 0.2 mm in the night heron's egg to 0.75 mm in the common murre's.

- **Not all eggs are oval** – those of owls and toucans are round, and auks lay pear-shaped eggs.

▲ *A bird's egg, though seemingly fragile, contains everything that the growing embryo inside needs to survive.*

Crows

- **Members of the crow family** live on all continents of the world, except Antarctica. There are about 117 species, including jackdaws, rooks, ravens, nutcrackers, choughs and jays, as well as common crows.

- **Bold and aggressive**, a typical crow is a big bird with a strong body and legs, and a powerful beak that can deal with nuts, seeds and even small prey.

- **At 66 cm long**, the raven is the largest of the crow family, and the largest of the songbird group of birds.

- **Crows** are thought to be among the most intelligent of all birds. Studies on ravens have shown that they are able to count up to five or six.

- **When food is plentiful**, nutcrackers hide nuts and pine seeds in holes in the ground, and are able to find them again months later.

- **There are many superstitions** about ravens – the arrival of a raven is said to be an evil omen and a sign of an imminent death.

- **A species of crow** that lives on the Pacific island of New Caledonia uses tools such as hooked twigs and sharp-ended stems to extract grubs from the crowns of palm trees.

- **Breeding pairs** of Australian white-winged choughs use a team of up to 8 other choughs to help them find food for their young.

- **Some crows in Japan** have learned how to get cars to crack nuts for them. They put the nuts in front of cars at traffic lights, wait for the cars to pass over them, and collect the kernels once the lights are red again!

★ **STAR FACT** ★
Magpies steal the eggs and young of other birds, as well as bright, shiny objects such as jewellery, which they hide in their nests.

▼ *The secret of the crows' success is their adaptability. They eat a wide range of foods and are intelligent enough to learn how to make use of new food sources. Shown here are: (1) the raven, (2) the rook, (3) the hooded crow,(4) the chough, (5) the jackdaw*

1

2

3

4

5

Old World sparrows

- **The house sparrow** originally came from Southwest Asia, but has spread throughout the world. It feeds mainly on seeds, but also eats some insects and is happy to eat scraps put out on bird tables.

- **Chestnut sparrows** drive other birds from their nests and use the nests themselves, instead of making their own.

- **The snow finch** lives high in mountain ranges and makes its nest on mountain ledges at altitudes of 5000 m.

- **All the house sparrows in the USA** are descended from a few birds that were released in Central Park, New York, in 1850.

▶ *There may now be as many as 150 million house sparrows in the USA.*

> ★ STAR FACT ★
> Sparrows like to bathe and splash in water, and will even bathe in snow in winter.

- **House sparrows** generally have two broods a year of 4–7 eggs each.

- **The desert sparrow** makes a nest of dry grass and twigs, often in a wall, and lays 2–5 eggs.

- **Most sparrows** are about 14–18 cm long and have brownish or grey plumage.

- **The 40 or so species of Old World sparrow** live in Europe, Africa and parts of Asia, though some have been introduced elsewhere.

- **House sparrows** rarely nest away from human habitation.

Auks

- **The Atlantic puffin's colourful beak** is striped red, yellow and grey blue, and can hold 12 or more fish.

- **The ancient murrelet** is so-named because it develops fine white feathers on its head in the breeding season, said to look like the white hairs of an elderly person.

- **The common guillemot** nests on narrow cliff ledges. Its eggs are pointed, so that if they get knocked, they roll in a circle and do not fall off.

- **The guillemot** can dive in water to a depth of 180 m as it hunts for fish.

- **The auk family** includes 22 species of diving birds,

▶ *The tufted puffin lives in the Arctic and North Pacific.*

including auks, guillemots, puffins and razorbills. They live in and around the North Pacific, Atlantic and Arctic oceans.

- **The common guillemot** is the largest of the auks, at about 45 cm long and 1 kg in weight. The least auklet is the smallest auk, at 16 cm long and 90 g.

- **Common guillemots** nest in colonies of thousands, with as many as 70 pairs occupying 1 sq m.

- **The little auk** nests in a cliff crevice and lays 1–2 eggs, which both parents incubate.

- **Auk eggs** are reputed to taste good, and have long been collected and eaten by humans.

> ★ STAR FACT ★
> The puffin flies at up to 64 km/h, with its wings beating 300–400 times a minute.

Bee-eaters and relatives

- **The 5 species of tody** are all insect-eating birds that live in the Caribbean islands.

- **Bee-eaters catch a bee or wasp** and kill it by striking it against a branch. Before eating it, the bird rubs the insect against the branch to expel its venom.

- **The blue-crowned motmot** has 2 long tail feathers with racquet-shaped tips. As the bird sits watching for prey, it swings its tail like a clock's pendulum.

- **Motmots** range in size from the 19-cm long tody motmot to the 53-cm long upland motmot.

- **Motmots lay their eggs** in a chamber at the end of a burrow dug in an earth bank. Both parents incubate the eggs and feed the chicks.

> ★ STAR FACT ★
> A European bee-eater eats about 200 bees a day. Its summer diet is mainly bumblebees, and in winter it eats honeybees and dragonflies.

- **The 27 species of bee-eater** are colourful birds that live in southern Europe, Africa, Asia and Australia.

- **The European bee-eater** flies some 16,000 km between Europe, where it breeds, and Africa, where it overwinters.

- **Todies** nest in 30-cm long tunnels, which they dig with their beaks.

- **The 10 species of motmot** live only in forests from Mexico to northern Argentina.

◀ *The white-fronted bee-eater lives in southern Africa.*

Warblers

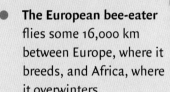

- **The willow warbler** is only 11 cm long, but flies all the way from northern Europe and Siberia to Africa to spend the winter – a distance of some 12,000 km.

- **The rarely seen grasshopper warbler** has an extraordinary whirring song and can 'throw its voice' like a ventriloquist.

▶ *At 19 cm long, the great reed warbler is larger than most European warblers.*

- **The warbler family** has more than 380 species. Most live in Europe, Africa, Asia and Australasia, but there are a few species in North and South America.

- **Most warblers** are 9–16 cm long, but the two largest – the South African grassbird and the Australian songlarks – are up to 23 cm long.

- **The Aldabra warbler**, discovered in 1967, lives only on a small part of Aldabra Island in the Indian Ocean. It has not been seen since 1983, so may well be extinct.

- **Insects** are the main food of most warblers, but they also eat some fruits, berries and seeds.

- **The marsh warbler** can mimic about 80 other species.

- **Chiffchaffs and willow warblers** look almost exactly alike, but their songs are quite different.

- **The blackcap** lays 4–6 eggs in a neat, cup-shaped nest. Both parents incubate them for 10–15 days.

- **The tailorbird** makes a cradlelike nest from two leaves sewn together with plant fibres or spiders' webs.

Pheasants and relatives

- **Domestic chickens** are descended from the red jungle fowl, which was first domesticated 5000 years ago. The jungle fowl still lives wild in Southeast Asia.

- **All 49 species of wild pheasant** are from Asia, except the Congo peafowl, which was first discovered in a Central African rainforest in 1936.

- **To attract females**, the male great argus pheasant dances and spreads out his enormously long wing feathers, like glittering fans.

- **The peacock's wonderful train** contains about 200 shimmering feathers, each one decorated with eyelike markings. When courting, he spreads the train and makes it 'shiver' to attract a female.

- **The Himalayan monal pheasant** spends some of the year above the tree line, where it has to dig in the snow with its beak to find insects and other food.

- **The male pheasant** mates with several females, each of which lays up to 15 eggs in a shallow scrape on the ground. The females incubate the eggs and care for the young by themselves, with no help from the male.

- **Most pheasants** nest on the ground, but the 5 species of tragopan, which live in tropical forests in Asia, nest in trees, often taking over the old nests of other birds.

- **The common pheasant** comes from Asia, but is now common in Australia, North America and Europe, where it is shot for sport.

- **In ancient Rome**, peacocks were roasted and served in their feathers as a great delicacy.

◀ The peacock is a native of India, Sri Lanka and Pakistan, but it has been introduced in many areas throughout the world. Only the male has the spectacular tail, which does not reach its full glory until the bird is about 3 years old. It may continue to grow for another 2–3 years.

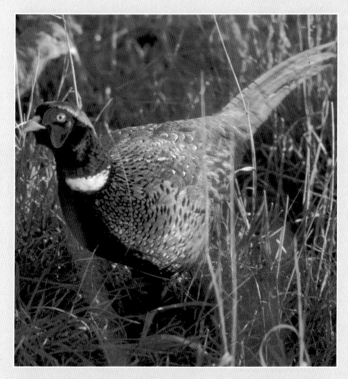

▲ The male pheasant is a beautiful bird with iridescent plumage on his head and bright red wattles. Originally from Asia, this pheasant has been successfully introduced in Europe and North America, where it is very common.

Manakins and cotingas

- **Manakins** are small birds that live in Central and South America. There are about 57 species.

- **Female manakins** do all the nesting work alone – they build the nest, incubate the eggs and care for the young.

- **The largest of the cotingas** is the Amazonian umbrellabird, which gets its name from the crest of feathers that hangs over its head.

- **The three-wattled bellbird** (cotinga family) is best known for its extremely loud call, which resounds through its jungle home.

- **Two of the most colourful South American birds** are the Guianan cock of the rock, which is bright orange, and the Andean cock of the rock, which is red (both cotinga family species).

- **Cocks of the rock** perform remarkable courtship displays – up to 25 male birds leap and dance together, fanning their feathers and making loud calls.

- **The 65 or so cotinga species** live in the forests of Mexico, some Caribbean islands and Central and South America.

- **Fruit and insects** are the main foods of both manakins and cotingas.

- **The female cock of the rock** makes a nest of mud and plants attached to a rock or cave wall, and incubates her eggs alone.

- **In his courtship display**, the male wire-tailed manakin brushes the female's chin with his long, wirelike tail feathers.

◀ *The little wire-tailed manakin lives in the lower levels of the Amazonian rainforest.*

New World vultures

- **There are 7 species of New World vultures** in North and South America. Like Old World vultures, their diet includes carrion.

- **New World vultures** lay their eggs on the ground or on a cliff ledge. The parent birds feed their young on regurgitated food.

- **Unusually colourful** for a bird of prey, the king vulture has bright red, orange and yellow bare skin and wattles on its head.

- **The king vulture** has a particularly good sense of smell, and can find carrion even in dense rainforest.

- **The turkey vulture** does not make a nest, but lays its 1–3 eggs on a cliff ledge or in a cave. Both parents help to incubate the eggs for up to 41 days.

- **Black vulture chicks** are looked after by both parents. They do not fly until they are 11 weeks old.

- **Vultures can go for weeks without food.** When they do find carrion, they eat as much as possible.

- **King vultures** have stronger beaks than other New World vultures, and are able to tear apart large animals.

- **The last wild California condors** were captured for captive breeding. By 1998 there were 170 birds, 50 of which were released into the wild.

- **The largest of all birds of prey** is the Andean condor, with a wingspan of more than 3 m.

◀ *The Andean condor soars for hundreds of kilometres over the Andes mountains, searching for food such as dead deer.*

Shearwaters and petrels

- **The shearwater's legs** are placed far back on its body, making it an expert swimmer, but preventing it from standing up properly. It moves awkwardly on land and has to launch itself from a tree into the air.

- **Unlike most birds**, shearwaters and petrels have a good sense of smell. They have long, tube-shaped nostrils on the tops of their beaks.

- **Shearwaters and petrels** are not tuneful birds, and at night the colonies make a very loud, harsh noise.

- **The 56 or more species** in the shearwater family include petrels, fulmars and prions. They range from the Antarctic to the Arctic.

- **Largest of the shearwater family** are the giant petrels, which at 99 cm long are almost the size of albatrosses.

▶ *Manx shearwaters nest in colonies of thousands of birds on offshore islands or isolated cliff tops.*

- **Fish and squid** are the main food of shearwaters, but giant petrels also feed on carrion, and can rip apart whales and seals with their powerful beaks.

- **The manx shearwater** lays 1 egg in a burrow. The male and female take turns at incubating it and feeding one another.

- **Young shearwaters** are fed on a rich mixture of regurgitated fish and squid, and may put on weight so quickly that they are soon heavier than their parents.

- **Prions** feed on tiny plankton, which they filter from the water through comblike structures at the sides of their beaks.

> ★ STAR FACT ★
> To defend themselves, shearwaters can spit out food and fish oil to a distance of 1 m.

Cassowaries and kiwis

- **There are 3 species of kiwi**, found only in New Zealand. All are flightless birds that live in burrows.

- **The female dwarf cassowary**, or moruk, is an extremely dangerous bird and will attack anything that comes near its nest with its 10-cm long claws.

- **The 3 species of cassowary** live in rainforests in New Zealand and northeastern Australia.

> ★ STAR FACT ★
> A kiwi lays the largest eggs for its size of any bird – each egg weighs 25% of its body weight. Females lay up to 100 in a lifetime.

- **Largest of its family is the brown kiwi**, which is about 55 cm long and weighs up to 3.5 kg.

- **Only the kiwi has nostrils** at the end of its beak.

- **The kiwi** is the national symbol of New Zealand, appearing on stamps, coins and banknotes.

- **Cassowaries in Australia** are known to eat the fruits of 75 different types of tree.

- **The female cassowary** mates with several males, laying 6–8 eggs each time. The males care for the young.

- **About 1200 years ago** there were probably 12 million kiwis in New Zealand. Today there are only 70,000.

◀ *The kiwi detects worms, insects and spiders using its sense of smell.*

Storks

- **In tropical areas**, storks' nests perched high on buildings can get very warm, so parents cool their young by regurgitating a shower of water over them.

- **The huge beak** of the whale-billed stork, or shoebill, is 23 cm long and 10 cm wide. It uses it to catch lungfish, young crocodiles and turtles.

- **The white stork** has long been a symbol of fertility in Europe. Parents used to tell their children that new babies were brought by a stork.

- **The 17 species of stork** live in North and South America, Europe, Africa, Asia and Australia.

- **Marabou storks** often scavenge on rubbish tips.

- **The openbill stork's beak** meets only at the tip. This helps it to hold its favourite food – large snails.

- **The tail feathers** of marabou storks were once used to trim hats and dresses.

- **When the wood stork's partly open beak** touches a fish under water, it snaps shut in 25 milliseconds –

one of the fastest reactions of any animal.

- **Male and female white storks** take turns to incubate their clutch of 3–5 eggs. When the partners change shifts, they perform a special bill-clattering display.

- **The adjutant stork** is named after the adjutant army officer, because of its stiff, military-style walk.

▼ *The saddlebill stork of southern Africa is easily recognized by its large red, yellow and black bill.*

Gulls and relatives

- **The great skua** is a pirate – it chases other birds and forces them to give up their prey in mid air.

- **The snowy sheathbill** scavenges for food on Antarctic research bases, and also steals eggs and chicks from penguin colonies.

- **There are about 48 species of gull** found on shores and islands all over the world.

- **Arctic glaucous and ivory gulls** sometimes feed on the faeces of marine mammals.

- **At up to 79 cm long**, the great black-backed gull is the giant of the group. The little gull is one of the smallest, at 28 cm long.

- **The Arctic explorer** James Clark Ross discovered Ross's gull in the 19th-century.

- **Skuas**, also called jaegers usually lay 2 eggs in a shallow, moss-lined nest on the ground. Both parents incubate the eggs and feed the young, which can fend for themselves by about 7 weeks old.

- **The kittiwake** spends much more time at sea than other gulls, and usually only comes to land in the breeding season. It has very short legs and rarely walks.

- **Herring gulls** have learned that they can find food in seaside towns, and many now nest on roofs instead of cliff ledges.

- **The south polar skua** lays 2 eggs, but the first chick to hatch usually kills the second.

▲ *Gulls eat a wide range of food, including fish, shellfish, the young of other seabirds and waste from fishing boats.*

Jacamars and relatives

- **Jacamars nest in tunnels** made in the ground or in termite mounds. They lay 2–4 eggs, which they incubate for 20–23 days.

- **Brightly coloured barbets** live in tropical forests and woodlands in Africa, Asia and South America.

- **At 30 cm long**, the great jacamar is the largest of the 17 species of jacamar. Its beak alone is almost 5 cm long.

- **The white-fronted nunbird** (puffbird family) digs a nesting burrow about 1 m long. The bird lays its eggs in a chamber at the end of the burrow.

- **Biggest of the 75 species of barbet** is the

▶ *The crested barbet of southern Africa usually searches for food on the ground.*

toucan barbet, at 20 cm long. It lives in mountain forests in the northern part of South America.

- **The double-toothed barbet** lays 3–4 eggs, usually in a tree hole. Both parents incubate the eggs and care for the young.

- **A jacamar** snaps up an insect in the air, then returns to its perch and bangs the insect against a branch to kill it before eating it.

- **There are about 33 species of puffbird** living in Mexico and Central and South America.

- **Barbet pairs** sing together to keep their relationship close. One bird starts to sing, then stops, and the other bird continues the song within a fraction of a second.

Drongos and relatives

- **The huia**, a species of wattlebird, has not been seen since 1907 and is probably extinct. It was noted for having a different shaped beak in males and females – the male's was straight and strong, the female's slender and curved.

- **The greater racquet-tailed drongo** has two long, wirelike tail feathers with twisted tips that make a humming noise as the bird flies.

- **The pied currawong** (Australian butcherbird family) attacks other birds and takes their young from their nests.

- **The 25 species of Old World oriole** live in Europe and parts of Asia, Africa and Australia. They are mainly tree-dwellers, feeding on insects and fruit.

- **There are 2 surviving species** of the wattlebird family – the kokako and the wattlebird, both of which live in New Zealand and rarely fly.

- **The golden oriole** makes a neat, cup-shaped nest that it binds to two supporting twigs. It lays 3–4 eggs.

- **Australia and New Guinea** are home to the 10 species of insect-eating bell-magpies.

- **Australian mud-nesters** work together to build nests of mud on the branches of trees.

- **The figbird** (oriole family) is a forest fruit-eater, but is now also common in towns.

- **Wood swallows**, found in Australasia and Southeast Asia, feed mostly on insects, but also drink nectar.

◀ *A common bird in southern Africa, the fork-tailed drongo has distinctive bright red eyes.*

Ibises and relatives

- **The ibis** was a symbol of the god Thoth in ancient Egypt, and appears in many paintings and carvings. Mummified ibises have also been discovered – as many as 500,000 in one tomb.

- **The spoonbill's beak** has a spoon-shaped tip that it uses to search shallow water for fish and small creatures.

- **At 1.4 m long** and weighing about 4 kg, the greater flamingo is the largest of the 5 species of flamingo.

- **The flamingo feeds** by forcing mud and water through bristly plates at each side of its beak with its tongue. Tiny creatures, algae and other food particles are trapped and swallowed.

- **Until their beaks have developed fully**, young flamingos feed on a 'milky' substance from their parents' throats.

- **The 31 species of ibis and spoonbill** live in North and South America, southern Europe, Asia, Africa and Australia, often in wetlands.

- **The glossy ibis** makes its nest in a reedbed or tree, and lays 3–4 eggs. The female does most of the incubation, but the male helps to rear the young.

- **Young flamingos** have grey feathers at first. Adult birds get their pink colour from pigments in the algae that they eat.

- **The greater flamingo** has a wingspan of 140–165 cm.

Beak for filtering food from water

Long neck allows the bird to feed in deep water

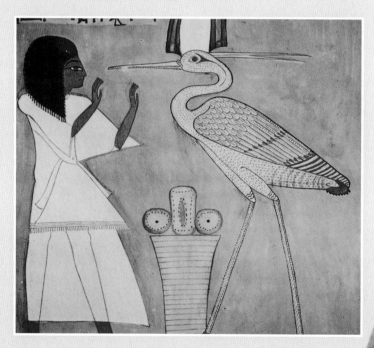

▲ The ancient Egyptian moon god Thoth was sometimes shown in paintings as an ibis, or as a human figure with the head of an ibis.

▶ The greater flamingo lives in huge flocks around lakes and deltas in Europe, Asia, parts of Africa, the Caribbean and Central America. It can live to be at least 50 years old.

Rheas and tinamous

- **The largest bird in South America** is the greater rhea, which stands 1.5 m tall and weighs up to 25 kg.

- **The 45 or so species of tinamou** all live in South America.

- **Most tinamous can fly**, if only for short distances, but they tend to run or hide rather than take to the air.

- **Female tinamous** lay eggs in the nests of more than one male. Males incubate the eggs and feed the chicks.

- **Rheas** feed mostly on plants, but will also eat insects and even lizards when they can.

- **Tinamous generally eat fruit**, seeds and other plant matter, but some species also gobble up insects.

- **Rheas live in flocks** of between 5–50 birds.

- **Rhea feathers** are used to make feather dusters, for sale mainly in the USA and Japan.

- **If threatened**, a rhea lies flat on the ground with its head stretched out in an attempt to hide.

◀ Flocks of rheas live on the pampas grasslands and in open woodland in southeastern South America.

Gannets and boobies

- **The gannet plunges 30 m or so** through the air and dives into the water to catch prey such as herring and mackerel.

- **A specially strengthened skull** helps cushion the impact of the gannet's high-speed dive into water.

- **Boobies** were given their common name because they were so easy for sailors to catch and kill.

- **The male blue-footed booby** attracts a mate by dancing and holding up his brightly coloured feet as it struts about.

- **When a gannet** comes to take its turn

incubating the egg, it presents its mate with a piece of seaweed, which is added to the nest.

- **There are 3 species of gannet and 6 species of booby**. Boobies generally live in tropical and subtropical areas, while gannets live in cooler, temperate parts of the world.

- **The gannet** usually lays just 1 egg, which both partners help to incubate for 43–45 days. They feed their chick with regurgitated food for up to 13 weeks.

- **Young gannets and boobies** are kept warm on their mother's feet for their first few weeks.

- **Boobies** spend most of their time at sea, only landing to breed and rear their young.

- **At up to 86 cm long** and with a wingspan of 152 cm, the masked booby is the largest of the boobies.

◀ Blue-footed boobies usually feed close to the seashore, while red-footed boobies venture further out to sea.

Pelicans

- **The great white pelican** catches about 1.2 kg of fish a day in its large throat pouch.

- **The brown pelican** dives from a height of 15 m above the water to catch fish below the surface.

- **Great white pelican breeding colonies** may number as many as 30,000 pairs of birds.

- **There are 7 species of pelican**. Most live and feed around fresh water, but the brown pelican is a seabird.

- **One of the largest pelicans** is the Australian pelican, which is up to 180 cm long and weighs about 15 kg.

- **The white pelican** lays 1–2 eggs in a nest mound on the ground. Both parents help to incubate the eggs and care for the young.

- **Pelican chicks** are able to stand at 3 weeks old and can fly at 7–10 weeks old.

- **In heraldry**, a pelican is often shown pecking its breast to feed its young on its blood. This myth may come from the bird's habit of resting its beak on its breast.

- **White pelicans work as a group** to herd fish into a shoal by swimming in a horseshoe formation. Then they scoop up pouchfuls of fish with their large beaks.

- **When flying**, a pelican flaps its wings 1.3 times a second.

◀ A great white pelican comes in to land on the water.

Buzzards, kites and osprey

- **Bees and wasps**, their larvae and even their nests are the main food of honey buzzards, which remove the stings from adult insects before eating them.

- **The snail kite's hook-tipped beak** is perfectly shaped for extracting the soft flesh of snails from their shells.

- **One of the most common of all birds of prey** is the black kite, which lives throughout most of Europe, Africa, Asia and Australia.

- **Osprey parents** stop feeding their young when it is time for them to leave the nest.

- **When fishing**, the osprey plunges into water feet first and grasps its slithery prey with its spine-covered feet.

- **The red kite** often takes over the old nest of a raven.

- **The rough-legged buzzard** is common over open tundra in the far north. It preys on rodents and rabbits.

- **A buzzard can spot a rabbit** popping up out of its burrow from more than 3 km away.

- **Male ospreys** feed the whole family once the chicks have hatched.

◀ The osprey's body measures 55–58 cm long, and it has an impressive 1.6-m wingspan. The females are slightly larger than the males.

★ STAR FACT ★
The osprey was described by Aristotle as early as 350 BC in his *Natural History*.

Toucans and honeyguides

- **At 61 cm long**, the toco toucan is the largest toucan. Its colourful beak alone is up to 20 cm long.

- **Although a toucan's beak is large**, it is not heavy. The beak is made of a lightweight material with a honeycomb structure.

- **The black-throated honeyguide** likes to feed on bees and their larvae. When it finds a bees' nest, it leads another creature, such as a honey badger, to the nest and waits while the animal breaks into the nest to feed on the honey. The honeyguide then has its share.

- **There are about 40 species of toucan.** They live in Mexico, Central and South America.

- **Toucans feed mostly on fruit,** which they pluck from

Beak is about
20 cm long and
7.5 cm deep at
the base.

Strong claws
for perching

▶ The black-throated
honeyguide is usually a quiet
little bird, but it chatters noisily
when it wants to attract a
helper, such as a honey badger,
to a bees' nest, so it can have a
share of the honey.

branches with their long beaks. They also eat some insects and small animals such as lizards.

- **Toucans** usually nest in tree holes. The female lays 2–4 eggs, and the male helps with the incubation, which takes about 15 days.

- **There are about 15 species of honeyguide.** Most live in forests and woodlands in Africa, but there are a few species resident in Asia.

- **Many honeyguides** lay their eggs in the nests of other birds, such as woodpeckers. When they hatch, the young honeyguides kill the young of the host bird.

- **Toucans are noisy creatures** – their loud squawks can be heard nearly 1 km away.

◀ The toco toucan of Brazil is the largest and best-known of the toucans. It sometimes perches on a branch near another bird's nest to steal the eggs or chicks. Intimidated by the toucan's great beak, the parent bird will not generally attack. When it sleeps, the toucan turns its head to rest its long beak along its back, and folds its tail over its head.

Woodpeckers

- **The woodpecker feeds** by drilling into tree bark with its sharp beak and then inserting its long tongue into the hole to pick out insects living beneath the bark.

- **Woodpeckers drum** on tree trunks with their beaks to signal their ownership of territory or their readiness to mate. The greater spotted woodpecker has been timed making 20 strikes a second.

- **The 200 or so species of woodpecker** live all over the world, except in Antarctica and the far north.

- **The imperial woodpecker**, at 55 cm long, is the biggest of its family. The little scaled piculet, by contrast, is only 8 cm long.

- **Woodpeckers** nest in holes in trees. They may use a hole from a previous year, or dig out a new one for their 2–12 eggs.

- **The woodpecker's tongue** is well-adapted for catching insects. It is so long that the woodpecker can stick it out beyond the tip of its beak, and its sticky coating easily mops up its prey.

- **The sapsucker** (woodpecker family) feeds on sweet, sugary sap. It bores a hole in a tree and laps up the sap that oozes out.

- **As well as insects**, the great spotted woodpecker eats the eggs and young of other birds.

- **A woodpecker** may eat up as many as 1000 ants in one feeding session.

- **During autumn**, the acorn woodpecker of North America bores as many as 400 holes in tree trunks and puts an acorn in each one, to store for the winter.

◀ *This great spotted woodpecker is sharing a feeder with a siskin. It lives in Europe, parts of Asia and North Africa.*

Grassland birds

★ **STAR FACT** ★
A fast walker, the long-legged secretary bird of the African grasslands may travel 30 km a day in search of snakes, insects and birds.

- **The yellow-billed oxpecker** of the African grasslands sits on buffaloes' backs, pulling ticks from their skin.

- **Flocks of 1 million or more red-billed quelea** are seen moving like vast clouds over southern Africa.

- **The grasslands of South America** are home to the red-legged seriema, a long-legged, fast-running bird that eats anything it can find, including snakes.

- **Unlike most hornbills**, the southern ground hornbill of southern Africa spends most of its time on the ground.

- **One of the biggest creatures** on the South American pampas is the rhea, which feeds mainly on grass.

- **Cattle egrets** accompany large grassland mammals, feeding on the insects that live on or around them.

- **The crested oropendola** is a grassland bird of South America. It hunts insects and other small creatures.

- **North America's largest owl**, the great horned owl, includes other grassland birds such as quail in its diet.

- **The western meadowlark** makes a ground nest of grass and pine needles in prairie grasslands.

▼ *Secretary birds are often seen perching and nesting in acacia trees.*

Monarchs and relatives

- **Monarch flycatchers** feed mainly on insects, darting out to catch them in the air and then taking them back to a perch to eat.

  - **The male African paradise flycatcher's tail feathers** are up to 20 cm long – much longer than its body.

  - **Only 7 Chatham Island robins** (Australasian robin family) were thought to exist in 1976, but a breeding programme using the Chatham Island tit to foster eggs has helped increase the population.

  - **There are about 90 species of monarch flycatchers.** They live in wooded areas in Africa, Southeast Asia, Australia and some Pacific islands.

▲ *The paradise flycatcher makes a neat nest of plant roots held together with spiders' webs on a slender branch or twig.*

> ★ STAR FACT ★
> Fantails are so-named because they continually fan their long tails from side to side.

- **The yellow-breasted boatbill**, a monarch flycatcher, has a broad beak with a hooked tip, which it uses to pick small insects off leaves.

- **Smallest of the Australasian robin family** is the rose robin, at 10 cm long and weighing only 10 g.

- **The black-naped blue monarch** lays 3–4 eggs in a nest of grass and bark bound together with spiders' webs. The nest is usually built on a forked branch.

- **In aboriginal folklore**, the willie wagtail (a fantail), was thought to be a gossipy bird that spread secrets.

- **The pied fantail's beak** is ringed with bristles that may help the bird to trap insect prey.

Megapodes and guans

- **The 12 species of megapodes** are ground-living birds found in Australia and some Pacific islands.

- **The mallee fowl** (a megapode) lays her eggs in a huge mound of rotting leaves and sand, which acts as an incubator. The mound can be up to 11 m across and 5 m high.

- **The male mallee fowl** checks the temperature of his nest mound with its beak and keeps it a constant 33°C by adding or removing material.

- **Mallee fowl chicks** must dig their way out of their nest mound, and are able to fly a few hours later.

- **To attract females**, as it flies the male crested guan flaps his wings briefly at more than twice the normal speed, making a whirring sound.

- **One megapode in Tonga** makes a nest of hot volcanic ash, which keeps its eggs warm.

- **The 45 species of guan and curassow** live from the southern USA to northern Argentina.

- **The great curassow** is 95 cm long and weighs 4.8 kg.

- **True to its name**, the nocturnal curassow comes out at night to sing and feed on fruit.

- **The plain chachalaca** (curassow family) lays 3 eggs in a nest made of sticks and lined with leaves and moss.

- **Now rare**, the white-winged guan lives in the Andean foothills, feeding on fruit, berries, leaves and insects.

▼ *The male mallee fowl keeps a constant watch on its nest.*

Owls

- **Owls** range in size from the least pygmy owl, at only 12–14 cm long, to the Eurasian eagle owl, at 71 cm.

- **The burrowing owl** nests in burrows in the ground, either digging its own with its strong claws, or taking over the burrows of animals such as prairie dogs.

- **The soft, fluffy edges of an owl's feathers** help to reduce flight noise, so it can hunt almost silently.

- **Female owls** are usually larger than males.

- **Owls swallow prey**, such as mice and insects, whole.

- **The female barn owl** lays 4–7 eggs, often in a tree hole.

- **The brown fish owl** has bare legs and feet – feathers would get clogged with fish scales.

- **The 151 or so species of owl** live in most parts of the world except the far north, New Zealand and Antarctica.

- **About 80 species of owl** hunt mostly at night.

- **Some Native Americans** believed that owls were the souls of people, and so should never be harmed.

▼ *Pel's fishing owl lives along riverbanks in parts of southern Africa.*

Buntings and tanagers

- **The little snow bunting** breeds in northern Greenland, further north than any other bird.

- **One tanager, the glossy flowerpiercer**, has a hooked, up-curved beak that it uses to pierce the bases of tubular flowers so it can feed on the nectar inside.

- **The 240 species in the tanager family** include flowerpiercers, honeycreepers and euphonias. All live in North and South America.

- **The male scarlet tanager** has bright red feathers in the breeding season, but in autumn his plumage changes to olive-green, similar to the female.

- **The western tanager** lines its nest of twigs and moss with fine roots and animal hair. The female incubates 3–5 eggs.

- **Some tanagers follow columns of army ants** in forests, and snap up the insects that flee the ants' path.

- **Seeds** are the main food of the dark-eyed junco (bunting family), although it does eat a few spiders.

- **The woodpecker finch** (a bunting) uses a fine twig or cactus spine as a tool to winkle out insects from holes.

- **The 13 species of finch** (bunting family) in the Galapagos Islands are probably all descended from the same ancestor, but have evolved different beak shapes and feeding habits depending on their environment.

- **The Galapagos finches** gave Charles Darwin important evidence for his theory of evolution.

◀ *The snow bunting spends summers in the Arctic, but flies south in winter.*

Hornbills

- **There are about 45 species of hornbill**, 25 in Africa and 20 in Southeast Asia. Most live among trees.

- **Hornbills range in size** from 38–165 cm. The largest of the family is the great Indian hornbill, and the smallest is the dwarf red-billed hornbill.

- **The eastern yellow-billed hornbill and the dwarf mongoose** have an unusual relationship – they help each other find food and watch out for predators.

- **The female great Indian hornbill** incubates her eggs in a tree hole, the entrance of which is walled up with chewed bark and mud. Through a slit-like opening in the wall, the male passes her food.

- **Hornbills keep the nest clean** by pushing any food waste and droppings out through the slit opening.

- **In parts of South Africa**, the southern ground hornbill is traditionally considered sacred, and is protected.

- **Fruit** is the main food of most hornbills, but the two ground hornbills catch and eat small animals.

- **All hornbills have large beaks**. In many species the beak is topped with a casque made of keratin and bone.

- **A male hornbill** may carry more than 60 small fruits at a time to his nest to regurgitate for its young.

- **Hornbills are the only birds** in which two neck vertebrae are fused, possibly to help support the beak's weight.

◀ The 50-cm long yellow-billed hornbill lives in southern Africa.

Bulbuls and relatives

- **The bearded greenbul** lives in African rainforests and has a beautiful whistling call that it uses to keep in touch with others of its species in the dense jungle.

- **Despite its small size**, the red-vented bulbul is an aggressive bird. In Asia, people sometimes bet on a male bird to win a fight against another male.

- **The yellow-vented bulbul** makes a nest of twigs, leaves and vine stems, often in a garden or on a balcony. Both parents incubate the 2–5 eggs and care for the young.

- **There are about 120 species of bulbul** found in Africa and southern Asia, usually in forests, although some bulbuls have adapted to built-up areas.

- **Bulbuls** range in

▲ The fairy bluebird spends most of its time looking for ripe fruit, especially figs.

size from 14–23 cm, and eat mainly insects and fruit.

- **The 2 species of fairy bluebirds** live in Asia, feeding on fruit, nectar and some insects.

- **Leafbirds** lay 2–3 eggs in a cup-shaped nest made in the trees.

- **The common iora** (a leafbird) scurries through trees searching the leaves for insects. It also sometimes eats mistletoe and other berries.

- **Male fairy bluebirds** have bright blue upperparts. Females are a dull greenish-blue with dark markings.

★ STAR FACT ★

When courting, the male common iora fluffs up its feathers, leaps into the air and tumbles back to its perch again.

Old World vultures

- **There are about 15 species of Old World vultures** living in southern Europe, Africa and Asia.

- **Unlike most birds of prey**, the palm-nut vulture is mostly vegetarian. Its main food is the husk of the oil palm fruit, although it also eats fish, frogs and other small creatures.

- **The Egyptian vulture** steals birds' eggs. It cracks the eggs by dropping them on the ground or throwing stones at them.

- **Most vultures are scavengers** rather than hunters – they feed on the carcasses of dead animals.

- **The lack of feathers** on a vulture's head means that it does not have to do lots of preening after it has plunged its beak deep into a carcass to feed.

- **Different species of vulture** eat different parts of a body – bearded vultures even eat the bones.

- **In hot weather**, some vultures cool down by squirting urine onto their legs – which can't smell nice!

▶ This Egyptian vulture is about to break open a thick-shelled ostrich egg with a stone so that it can eat the contents. The vulture also eats carrion – several birds may be seen circling above a dead or dying animal when they find one.

> ★ STAR FACT ★
> The bearded vulture drops bones from a great height to smash them. It then swallows the bone fragments, which are broken down by powerful acids in its stomach.

- **The female white-backed vulture** lays 1 egg in a large stick nest made high in a tree. She incubates the egg for 56 days, being fed by the male. Both parents feed and care for the chick.

- **The lappet-faced vulture** is the largest vulture in Africa – it measures about 1 m long and has a huge 2.8 m wingspan. It also has a bigger beak than any other bird of prey.

Hooked beak for pecking scraps of meat from bones

Stone raised to throw at egg to break it open

Herons and bitterns

- There are about 60 species of heron and bittern.

- **The largest of the heron family** is the goliath heron of Africa and southwest Asia – it measures 1.5 m long.

- **The loud booming call** made by the male bittern in the breeding season can be heard up to 5 km away.

- **The great blue heron** makes a platform nest of twigs,

▲ *The great egret catches fish and shellfish in shallow water.*

★ STAR FACT ★
The green-backed heron of Japan tempts fish with bits of 'bait' such as bread or feathers.

often high in a tree. The 4 eggs take 25–29 days to hatch.

- **Special feathers** on the heron's breast and rump crumble into a powdery substance that the bird rubs into its plumage to help remove dirt and fish slime.

- **The white feathers of the great egret** were popular hat decorations in the late 1800s – more than 200,000 birds were killed for their feathers in a single year.

- **Like most herons**, the grey heron feeds on fish and frogs, which it catches with swift stabs of its beak.

- **Cattle egrets** nest in colonies – there may be more than 100 nests close together in one tree.

- **When hunting**, the black heron holds its wings over its head like a sunshade. This may help the bird spot fish, or the patch of shade may attract fish to the area.

Hummingbirds

- **The bee hummingbird** is not much bigger than a bumblebee and, at 6 cm long, is probably the smallest bird.

- **A hummingbird** hovers in front of flowers to collect nectar with its tongue, which has a brushlike tip.

- **When a bee hummingbird hovers**, it beats its wings 200 times a second.

- **The 320 or so species of hummingbird** live in North, Central and South America. Largest is the giant hummingbird, at about 20 cm long and weighing 20 g.

- **At 10.5 cm**, the beak of the sword-billed hummingbird is longer than the rest of its body.

- **Aztec kings** used to wear ceremonial cloaks made of hummingbird skins.

▲ *The tiny bee hummingbird lives on the island of Cuba in the Caribbean.*

- **Tiny ruby-throated hummingbirds** migrate each autumn from the USA across the Gulf of Mexico to Central America. Although only 9 cm long, the bird flies at a speed of about 44 km/h.

- **The female calliope hummingbird** lays 2 tiny eggs in a nest made of lichen, moss and spiders' webs. She incubates the eggs for 15 days, and feeds the young for about 20 days until they are able to fly and find food for themselves.

- **Hummingbirds** are the only birds able to fly backwards as well as forwards while they are hovering.

- **A hummingbird** must eat at least half its weight in food each day to fuel its energy needs.

Nuthatches and relatives

- **The red-breasted nuthatch** paints the entrance of its tree hole nest with sticky pine resin. This may stop insects and other creatures getting into the nest, but the birds also have to take care not to get their own feathers stuck.

- **The wallcreeper** is an expert climber and can clamber up steep cliffs and walls in its search for insect prey. It lives high in mountains such as the Alps and Himalayas.

- **The treecreeper** supports itself with its stiff tail feathers as it moves up tree trunks feeding on insects and spiders.

- **The 24 or so species of nuthatch** live in North America, Europe, North Africa, Asia and Australasia.

- **The European nuthatch's 6–9 eggs** hatch after 14–18 days.

- **Insects and spiders** are the main food of nuthatches, but in autumn the birds store nuts and seeds for the winter.

- **There are 7 species** of treecreeper, 7 species of Australian creeper and 2 species of Philippine creeper.

- **The largest nuthatch** is the giant nuthatch, at up to 20 cm long.

- **The Kabylie nuthatch** was only discovered in 1975, on an Algerian mountain.

▲ The common treecreeper lives in woodland, parks and gardens in Europe and Asia.

> ★ STAR FACT ★
> Nuthatches are the only birds that can climb down trees head first, as well as up.

Finfoots and relatives

- **The sunbittern** gets its name from the rich red-orange markings on its wings.

- **The sungrebe** (finfoot family) has an unusual way of caring for its young. The male bird carries his chicks in two skin pouches beneath his wings while they complete their development, even flying with them.

- **The only species in its family**, the sunbittern lives in jungles and swamps in Central and South America.

- **The kagu** is a flightless bird that lives only on the Pacific island of New Caledonia.

- **Finfoots are aquatic birds** that feed in the water on fish, frogs and shellfish. There is one species each in Afric, Southeast Asia and Central and South America.

- **The 2 species of seriema** live in South America. They eat snakes, banging their heads on the ground to kill them.

- **Seriemas can fly**, but prefer to escape danger by running fast over the grassy plains where they live.

- **Much of the kagu's habitat** on the island of New Caledonia has been destroyed by nickel mining, and the bird is now very rare.

- **The sunbittern lays 2 eggs** in a tree nest made of leaves and plant stems. Both parents take turns to incubate the eggs and care for the chicks.

- **The sungrebe and finfoots** have lobed feet, which help them swim.

▶ A sunbittern shows off its beautiful plumage with its wings spread.

Desert birds

- **The little cinnamon quail-thrush** of Australia hides in a burrow during the day to escape the hot sun.

- **The verdin** lives in the deserts of Mexico and the southwest of the USA, where it makes its nest on a cactus plant.

- **With few trees and bushes to sit in**, desert birds spend most of their lives on the ground.

- **The mourning dove** is a desert bird of the southwestern USA. A fast flier, it often travels great distances to find food and water.

- **Turkey vultures** soar over the American desert searching for carrion to eat.

- **Insects** are a favourite food of many desert birds, but some catch small mammals and others eat seeds.

> ★ STAR FACT ★
> Desert-living bird species are usually smaller than those found elsewhere in the world.

- **Most desert birds** are active at dawn and towards sunset, resting in shade for much of the day.

- **Owls, poorwills and nightjars** cool down in the desert heat by opening their mouths wide and fluttering their throats.

- **The roadrunner** reabsorbs water from its faeces before it excretes them.

◀ *The greater roadrunner lives in the western USA, where it preys on snakes as well as insects and mice.*

Mesites and relatives

- **Mesites** are thrushlike birds that search for insects on the forest floor. They do have wings, but rarely fly.

- **There were 3 species of mesite in Madagascar**, but two have not been seen for years and may be extinct.

- **The 15 species of buttonquail** live in parts of Europe, Africa, Asia, Australia and some Pacific islands, usually on grassland. Although they look like quails, they are not related.

◀ *The little buttonquail lives in southern Europe, Africa and parts of Asia. It is 13–15 cm long.*

- **Shy little birds**, buttonquails lurk among low-growing plants feeding on seeds and insects.

- **The female buttonquail** is larger than the male. She mates with several males and leaves each to incubate the clutch of eggs and rear the young.

- **Buttonquails** are sometimes known as hemipode, or half-footed, quails, because they lack rear toes.

- **The plains-wanderer** lives on the dry plains of central Australia. If in danger, it stays very still.

- **Plains-wanderers** are now rare because so much of the grassland where they live and feed has been cleared for agriculture. There may be fewer than 8000 left in the wild.

- **The female plains-wanderer** lays 4 eggs, usually in a nest made in a hollow in the ground, but it is the male that incubates the eggs and rears the young.

- **Buttonquail young** can fly 2 weeks after hatching, and start to breed when only 4–5 months old.

Cuckoos and hoatzin

- **The greater roadrunner**, a type of cuckoo, can move at a speed of 20 km/h or more on land.

- **The Eurasian cuckoo** is a 'brood parasite' – it lays its eggs in the nests of other birds.

- **Most birds take several minutes to lay an egg**, but the cuckoo lays one in just 9 seconds, so it can quickly take advantage of any brief absence of the host bird.

- **Of the 129 or so species of cuckoo**, only about 50 lay their eggs in other birds' nests.

- **The 60-cm long hoatzin** (there is only one species) lives in South America's rainforest.

- **Hoatzin chicks** leave the nest soon after hatching. Two little claws on each wing help them clamber about.

- **The 22 species of turaco** live only in Africa. Largest is the 90-cm long great blue turaco, weighing 1 kg.

- **Turacos** feed mostly on fruit, leaves and flowers, but also catch some insects in the breeding season.

- **Amazingly, the eggs of brood parasite cuckoos** vary in colour and markings according to the host they use. A Eurasian cuckoo's eggs may resemble those of reed warblers, garden warblers or redstarts.

- **The Australian koel** prefers fruit to the caterpillars and other creatures eaten by other cuckoos.

▲ *These flycatchers are busy feeding a cuckoo chick in their nest.*

Pittas and relatives

- **Bright red, green or yellow eyes** characterize the 15 colourful species of broadbill, which live in parts of tropical Africa and Southeast Asia.

- **The brightly coloured pittas** live in Africa, Southeast Asia and Australia. 'Pitta' is an Indian word meaning 'bird' – it was first used in the 1700s.

- **The 4 species of asity** are found only in Madagascar.

- **Most broadbills** feed on insects, which they catch in the air. Some also eat lizards and frogs.

- **The 24 or so species of pitta** range in size from 15–25 cm.

> ★ STAR FACT ★
> Rainbow pittas put wallaby droppings in and around their nests to disguise their own smell and keep tree snakes away from their eggs.

- **The Indian pitta** makes a nest of moss and twigs. Both parents incubate the 4–6 eggs.

- **The wattled false sunbird** (asity family) gets its name from its long, sunbird-like beak. Like the sunbirds, it takes nectar from flowers.

- **The green broadbill** hangs its nest from a vine and covers it with lichen and spiders' webs.

- **Pittas are said to have the best sense of smell** of any songbird. This may help them find worms and snails in the dim light of the forest floor.

◀ *The hooded pitta (front) and red-bellied pitta live in tropical rainforests.*

Mousebirds and trogons

▶ The beautiful quetzal is becoming rare because much of its forest habitat in Central America has been destroyed.

- **The quetzal** is a species of trogon that lives in Central America. It was sacred to the ancient Maya and Aztec civilizations.

- **The male quetzal's beautiful tail feathers** are up to 1 m long.

- **Mousebirds** get their name from their habit of scurrying around on the ground like mice as they search for seeds and leaves to eat.

- **There are about 37 species of trogon** living in the forests and woodlands of Central America, the Caribbean islands and parts of Africa and Asia.

- **Trogons range in size** from the black-throated trogon, at 23 cm long, to the slightly larger resplendent quetzal, at 33 cm long not including the tail feathers.

- **The 6 species of mousebird** are all small, dull-coloured birds of about 10 cm in length. They live in Africa south of the Sahara.

- **Mousebirds are plant eaters**, feeding on a variety of leaves, buds, flowers and fruits.

- **Trogons nest in tree holes** or in old termite mounds or wasps' nests. Both parents incubate the 2 –4 eggs for 17–19 days, and both care for the young.

- **Insects** are the main food of the trogons, but some also eat fruit and catch creatures such as lizards.

> ★ STAR FACT ★
> The monetary unit of Guatemala is known as the quetzal, after the resplendent quetzal – the country's national bird.

Wood warblers and icterids

- **The crested oropendola**, an icterid, weaves a hanging nest that may be up to 1 m long. The birds nest in colonies, and there may be as many as 100 large hanging nests in one tree.

- **Like the cuckoo**, the female brown-headed cowbird lays her eggs in the nests of other birds. She may lay as many as 40 eggs a year.

- **Kirtland's warbler** has very specialized breeding needs – it nests only around jack pine trees that are up to about 6 m tall.

- **The 114 species of wood warbler** live in North, Central and South America.

▶ The yellow warbler can be found from chilly Alaska to tropical South America.

- **The bobolink** breeds in southern Canada and the USA and migrates to South America for the winter – the longest migration journey of any icterid.

- **Great-tailed grackles** (icterid family) are big, noisy birds that scavenge on rubbish as well as feeding on insects, grain and fruit. They are common in towns and villages.

- **The Baltimore oriole** is the state bird of Maryland, USA. A song named after the bird was written by Hoagy Carmichael in the 1930s.

- **Male icterids** are generally much larger than females. The male great-tailed grackle is as much as 60% heavier than the female.

- **The yellow warbler** lays 4–5 eggs in a nest of bark and plant fibres made in a tree.

- **Largest of the 92 species of icterid** is the olive oropendola, at 52 cm long.

Vireos and relatives

- **Plantcutters** get their name from their large, serrated beaks, used to chop leaves from plants.

- **The 3 species of plantcutter** live in southern South America. The birds are 17–20 cm long.

- **The sharpbill** of Central and South America picks tiny insects and spiders from leaves.

- **The 43 species of vireo** live in North, Central and South America, and range in size from 10–16 cm.

- **The black-capped vireo** usually attaches its nest to a forked twig. Both parents incubate the 3–5 eggs and feed the young.

- **Red-eyed vireo chicks** are naked and helpless when they hatch, but open their eyes after 4–5 days, and leave the nest after 12 days.

- **Insects** such as caterpillars and aphids are the main foods of vireos, but some species also eat fruit.

- **Vireos** take about a week to make their nest. The female makes a cup-shape of spiders' webs and silkworm threads around her body, and then adds plant material such as grass and moss to the nest.

- **When vireos were first named** in the 1800s, people thought they heard the word 'vireo', meaning 'I am green', in the birds' song. In fact most vireos are green.

- **The brown-headed cowbird** often lays its eggs in the nests of vireos, which sometimes throw out the cowbird's eggs.

◄ The red-eyed vireo breeds in North America in the summer.

Endangered birds

- **More than 80 species of parrot**, such as the hyacinth macaw, are in danger of extinction or are very rare.

- **At least 1000 bird species** now face extinction – 30 or so became extinct in the 1900s.

- **The Hawaiian mamo** (Hawaiian honeycreeper family) became extinct in 1899, partly because more than 80,000 birds were killed to make a cloak for King Kamehameha I.

- **There are only about 600 black-faced spoonbills left.**

★ STAR FACT ★

The bald eagle was threatened by the harmful effects of DDT on its eggs, but has recovered since the pesticide was banned in 1972.

- **The Fiji petrel** was first discovered on the island of Gau Fiji in 1855, and was not seen again until 1984. Numbers are thought to be low.

- **Possibly less than 1000** red siskins remain in the wild – it has been a popular cage-bird since the mid 1800s.

- **The Floreana mockingbird** disappeared from one of the Galapagos Islands because rats were introduced.

- **The short-tailed albatross** has long been exploited for its feathers, and has been extremely rare since 1930.

- **In New Zealand**, Hutton's shearwater is preyed on by introduced stoats, while deer trample its burrows.

◄ The hyacinth macaw has suffered from illegal hunting for the pet trade and from habitat destruction. It is now bred in captivity.

INDEX

Acknowledgements

Artists: L R Galante (Galante Studio), Roger Goringe, Alan Harris, Mike Hughes, Roger Kent (Illustration), Mick Loates (Linden Artists), Kevin Maddison, Steve Roberts, Eric Robson, Rudi Vizi

All photographs are from: MKP Archives; Corel Corporation; Digital Stock Corp; Digital Vision; PhotoDisk